Developing

Your

Vocabulary

Developing Your Vocabulary

A. Rae Price
Penn Valley Community College

WM. C. BROWN COMPANY PUBLISHERS
Dubuque, Iowa

Sixth Printing, 1978

Printed in the United States of America

Contents

Preface

Many people know more than they think they know about word study. For example, they know the word *homogenized* from their milk cartons. But they are unaware that the prefix **homo-** is the same as the prefix found in the words **homo**geneous and **homo**nym; or that the root **gene** is the same root as in **gene**tics, de**gene**rated, and **gene**rator.

If they were made aware of the word elements they already know, they could unlock the meanings of hundreds of new words.

> **ex-** as in **ex**-president meaning "out of office" added to **hume** as in **hum**us meaning "soil" gives **exhume** meaning "out of the soil"
>
> **sub-** as in **sub**way meaning "under" added to **poena** as in **pen**alty gives **subpoena** meaning "under penalty"

Students can profit from such awareness. For in college, as well as on their jobs, they will run into hundreds, even thousands, of new words that can be linked with word elements that they already know— or can easily learn.

Developing Your Vocabulary helps students identify and use common word elements—prefixes, roots, and suffixes—and helps students link these elements to form thousands of words. Thus, students become word analysts, learning to practice their analysis both in and out of the classroom.

Secondly, *Developing Your Vocabulary* helps students enjoy word study by giving them steps on how to learn and by encouraging them to learn words that interest them. Words used in psychology, business and law, health fields, the metric system, and foreign countries are among the categories included.

Among the unique features of the book are the word wheels and word pyramids, both of which visually aid the students in extending word recognition. A second feature is the Notes pages which are found on some left-hand pages throughout the book. These pages provide four additional items: supplementary information of special interest; answer keys for short check-up quizzes; words in context; and room for students to add their own questions, comments, and additional dictionary work if desired.

A final feature, already proven effective, is the use of a card system—Data Retention Cards. This system allows students to break words into manageable parts and reinforce their learning by repetition and practice.

Developing Your Vocabulary follows a simple format, ranging from the easiest to the more complex. Each chapter centers around a learning technique with exercises interspersed between short, conversational passages. Students may pace themselves, taking the master check-up quiz over each chapter when ready. These master check-up quizzes at the back of the book are on perforated pages for easy removal. Rounding out the helpful aids are a progress chart, master lists of word elements, and a complete index.

Why is such a text as *Developing Your Vocabulary* useful to students? Why should students continue to build their vocabularies? No measure of intelligence reveals more than the measure of one's vocabulary. Many beginning college students yearn for the tools to build better vocabularies. With a good working vocabulary, chances for success are increased and learning becomes more enjoyable.

Developing Your Vocabulary can help provide that good working vocabulary for your students and can help them keep on learning long after they have left the classroom.

Note to the Reader

You *want* to add new words to your vocabulary, or you would not be studying this book. But you may ask yourself as you study some of the words in this book: why should I know *these* words?

This text works with word elements that will be new *and* useful to you. Our basic English word list came from the peasant folk of England; they took words from many places and put them to work. About ninety percent of the words on this page came from the English peasants.

About 800 years ago soldiers, scholars, priests and rulers from the mainland of Europe began to invade England. From that time on, a rich over-lay of scholarly, scientific terms was added to the English language. These terms came primarily from the French, Latin, and Greek. Although not used in our conversations as frequently as the old English peasant words, these words must be learned in order to understand newspapers, magazines, and the scientific writings of our day. The majority of words to be studied in this text come from these French, Latin, and Greek bases. Be assured that these words will not be strange to you. Rather, as you continue to listen, study and discuss, their frequent appearance will amaze you.

These words appear in such diverse fields as business, psychology and medicine, law, electronics, and education. Being familiar with the vocabulary learned in this text can aid you no matter what field you choose for work or study.

How to Use This Book

An old Chinese proverb states:

> I hear and I wonder
> I see and I remember
> I do and I understand.

The more actively engaged you are in the learning process, the more you will learn. Active engagement includes writing, practicing aloud, sometimes reading. Active engagement includes *thinking*: running ideas through your head, putting things together in ways that are new to you, and linking what you want to learn to what you already know. This book encourages you to do these things and more.

First of all, thumb through the book. Read the table of contents; you will note that the chapters are built around learning techniques. Read the note to the reader; you will find out something about the type of words you will be learning in this text. Then flip quickly through the text, examining briefly the left-hand, N-numbered pages with their comments and clippings. Examine the appendix, the master list of word elements studied, the master quizzes, the sheet for recording your progress, the over-all index. The master quizzes and record sheet are on perforated pages for easy removal.

Five things are especially important to remember:

1. For the short quizzes throughout the book, answer keys are provided for you at the bottom of the left-hand pages. As you will learn or may already know, finding out immediately what you are doing right and what you need further work on is vital to learning. So *use* these answer keys to check yourself immediately. If you missed anything, correct yourself *then*.

2. You will find many other blanks to be filled in throughout the book in addition to the blanks on check-up quizzes. Be sure to fill

in all blanks as you go along. For example, you are asked in Chapter 2:

What does meditation mean? _____

You are to fill in the blank with a word or phrase that you think is a good synonym for the word "meditation." In this case, you can check yourself in the next sentence to see if you are correct.

3. Comments and clippings on some pages include *additional* material. You may follow through the entire text without them. The information on the left-hand pages is not essential for the check-up quizzes, although it often helps. You may want to work through a chapter without reading the comments and clippings, and then, as you review, pay special attention to them. Much material of interest is found on these pages; you will profit by either reading the left-hand pages as you go along, or going back over the chapter and reading them with your review.

4. Plenty of space is provided for *you* to make notes, ask questions, and practice what you are learning. You are encouraged throughout the book to use as many of your senses as possible in learning. For example: SAY WORDS ALOUD so that you can hear them as well as see them. WRITE WORDS DOWN as you think of them and wonder about them. Use the empty areas on the left-hand pages to ask yourself questions or check up on how much you remember. Practice words or word elements that you missed on quizzes as you go along. Writing a word 500 times is a waste of time; writing it four or five times is not. So USE the empty space. Your textbook—like your vocabulary—should have the stamp of YOU on it.

5. On the right-hand column of many pages, you will find the initials DRC with words under the initials. For example:

<u>DRC</u>
re-

You will be instructed to buy a set of 3 x 5 index cards and use them by writing a new word element on one side of a card, and the meaning and a sample usage on the other side. This technique (Data Retention Cards) will save you a great deal of time and will make it possible for you to learn at times and in places that otherwise might be lost.

To summarize:

1. Check the answers to the short quizzes as soon as you finish them; answer key is at bottom of left-hand page.

2. Fill in all the blanks; check your answers in the next sentence or so. If you did not get the correct answer, try to figure out why.

3. Read the comments and clippings on the left-hand pages either as you go through each chapter the first time or as you review.

4. Use the book—write in it, add further notes on the N-(Notes) pages jot down questions, write down additions to word elements you are studying. (When you learn that the prefix RE- means "back" or "again," you can write down on the left-hand page all the words you can think of using the prefix RE-: reward, rewrite, refinance, refinish. . . .)

5. Make Data Retention Cards (DRC) as suggested. Carry them around with you, practice, sort, add to and discard as you learn. Save yourself valuable time and learn more efficiently.

This book combines discussion with programmed learning. It asks you to practice often and gives you valuable tools for learning. You can apply these tools in many areas of learning. So engage yourself actively as you use this book.

6. **NOTE:** Your **auditory** sense, or your hearing, is what you use in the **auditorium.** Then what's an **audit?** It once meant a "hearing," but now means an examination of records for accuracy.

Learn How to Learn

1. What marks the educated person? Why does one man move up in the business world while another fails to budge? Why is one woman looked up to, listened to, while another sinks back in greyness?

2. There are many reasons, of course. But a major reason, quite simply, is that some people possess a splendid command of language. They have a broad vocabulary; they know how to use it; and they have learned methods for increasing it.

3. No matter what shape your vocabulary is in now, you can improve it by becoming acquainted with, and applying, a few simple rules of learning. That's what this book is all about.

4. Looking up a list of 100 words in a dictionary is not a very effective learning device for most of us. We simply don't remember many words that way.

5. But recognizing frequently used prefixes and roots, some of which you already know, but may not *know* you know, does help. Making up new combinations with these word parts *does* work in understanding hundreds of words. Chapters 2 through 6 will help you do this.

6. Using as many of your senses as possible in expanding your word knowledge is another valuable technique. For example, use your **auditory** sense, or your hearing, to reinforce your new knowledge. Throughout this book, you will be encouraged to read words aloud. (Don't use this book only *in* the library.) Use this book when you can do one of the following.

  1. discuss the words with others
  2. hear yourself say the words

You will learn more about using various tools of learning, including your own senses, in Chapter 7.

ecried as the "desk
r to excoriate. Am
n modern times. t

mercury
e environment.
phere of the nort
record

12. **Spectrum,** a distribution or range of items closely related to each other, comes from the same base as many other words you know: spectator, spectacles, speculate, inspect; all of them have to do with "looking" or "seeing."

7. In Chapter 8, you will learn about the importance of studying things in which you are most interested; then in Chapter 9 you will be encouraged to experiment with words, putting them together in new ways, being creative. You can learn while you are waiting for someone to pass you the salt or while you are passing trucks on the freeway.

8. Each Chapter, 2 through 9, centers around a Learning Technique. These Learning Techniques can be useful to you in learning many things, but in this text you will use them to increase your vocabulary. But first of all, you need to learn *how* to learn. This first chapter concentrates primarily on setting the stage for learning.

9. There are two important points to keep in mind as you learn how to learn. The first is to expand your *learning environment*. What is your learning environment? This book, your instructors. Whatever you read and hear—from books to TV, from signboards to sermons. Whatever surrounds you makes up your environment. You can use this environment continually, examining words in a variety of contexts.

10. The first three chapters are closely related. Chapters 2 and 3 will help you:

Chapter 2: break words into manageable parts;
Chapter 3: consciously link the unknown to the known.

You will be amazed how much you already know, and thus you can begin immediately to expand your learning environment.

11. For example, you have just read ten paragraphs about your use of this text. Most of the words you probably knew, but you may not realize how *much* you knew about some of them. For example, you recognized:

educated   paragraph 1
expanding   paragraph 6
experiment   paragraph 7
expand   paragraph 9

12. All four start with the prefix e- or **ex-**. You know that **ex-** means "formerly," "out," or "out of," as in

expel or **ex-president**
or "That's my **ex.**"

Knowing that **ex-** means _____ or _____

_____ you can now use that knowledge in the following words.
(Fill in blanks)

    ex-officio: _____ ____ office

    excavate: to hollow _____

    excise: to cut _____ (also used as a kind of indirect tax: excise tax)

    exhume: to take _____ ____ the earth (humus)

    expatriot: a _____ patriot

    exorbitant: _____ ____ orbit, excessive

Check your responses with the answer key at the bottom of the page N-2. You can make a **spectrum** of words using **ex-**

You can probably add some others on your own; you can certainly spot that prefix **ex-** when you find it in your learning environment.

13. Here are two more words from the first ten paragraphs:

        vocabulary   paragraphs 2, 3
        dictionary   paragraph 4

Common words? Certainly. But you can expand word knowledge by studying them briefly.

14. Both refer to "words" or "speech." **Vocabulary** has the root **voc** in it, which means "to call." **Voc** can be recognized in such words as:

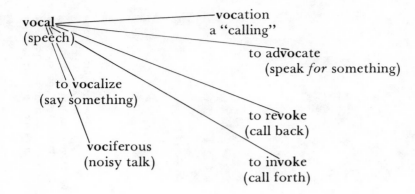

You could write.

"They **voc**iferously ad**voc**ated re**vok**ing the amendment, thus pro**vok**ing a tremendous outcry."

This means

They noisily spoke in favor of calling back the amendment, thus bringing forth a tremendous outcry.

vociferously	means noisily
advocated	means to speak in favor of something
revoking	means to call back
provoking	means bringing forth, producing, or stirring up

15. And **dictionary**? What can we do with it? Well, **dictionary**, of course, refers to a list of words and their meanings, pronunciation and so forth. **Diction** refers to "words" or "speech." If you have careful diction, you speak clearly, distinctly.

16. We use **diction** (or **dic**) in:

bene**dic**tion: good speech (usually at the close of a formal religious ceremony)

contra**dic**tion: to speak against ("Do not contradict your wife.")

dictate: to say aloud, to command ("The dictator is in the habit of dictating his letters.")

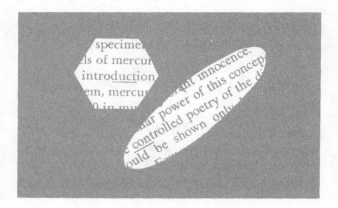

19. **NOTE:** The word conducive is very much like:

        conductor

        conduct

and simply means "leading toward," or "favoring." You will learn many other words using parts of this word: For example, the prefix **con-,** is in **con**nect, **con**note, **con**temporary; the root **duct** is in de**duct**, in**duct**ion, de**duct**ion, pro-**duct**ion, intro**duct**ion, ab**duct**, **duc**al, **duc**hy.

edict: to speak out formally ("The ruler handed down his edict.")

vindicate: to speak in favor of, to justify ("She was vindicated by the court's decision.")

17. Now, see how you are doing:

ex- means _____ ____, _____ or _____

vocal (voc) refers to _____ or _____

diction (dic) also refers to _____ or _____

Write in the blanks below the appropriate meanings from the list on the right.

exhume _____   a formal statement

ex-officio _____   speak in favor of something

advocate _____   justify

vindicate _____   take out of the earth

edict _____   loud, vehement talk

Check your responses with the answer key at the top of page N-6.

18. It's amazing. From three word elements, ex-, voc and dict, you have twenty-one words. And *many* more words that you now recognize use these word elements.

So you can expand your learning environment. You can analyze words wherever you are. Let's pre**dict** you will **voc**alize more freely with your new **ex**perience in analyzing words.

19. As has been stated, this kind of word analysis can take place wherever you have your thinking-motor turned on. But there is a second, more formal process in learning how to learn. Study in an atmosphere **conducive** to learning. Learn under conditions which are favorable, comfortable and non-aversive to you. For example:

(A) If you hate (check one or two)

_____ western music   _____ soul music

_____ rock music   _____ classical music

don't try to take a quiz over Chapter 2 while **that** music is on.

(B) If you can't study when (check one or more)

_____ TV is on   _____ you are hungry

_____ the room is too quiet   _____ you feel frustrated, up tight

don't try to think about some new prefixes when that condition prevails.

(C) If you are mad at or unhappy about   (anything) don't try to learn vocabulary terms while you are stewing. Go listen to some music or go work on your favorite hobby. But don't try to learn vocabulary.

20. In other words, pick your own place to learn. But don't make learning vocabulary a punishment, and don't use it as a dodge. There are lots of places where this book and its various devices can be used, from the breakfast table to the classroom to the pre-bed-time, brushing teeth time. But don't try to learn new words when a lot of things are working against you.

21. So you have two sub-points in learning how to learn:

   1. Expand your learning environment by analyzing words wherever you are, informally.
   2. Study in an atmosphere conducive to learning, when you get down to serious business.

   Now for the second part of this chapter.

22. Is your learning environment favorable? If not, change your setting. Or return to this section when it is favorable. This part is concentrated, so your atmosphere should be conducive to learning.

23. Earlier in this chapter six words appeared that are common in psychological studies.

Psychological Term	Used in Paragraph(s)	Meaning
reinforce	6	to strengthen, implant firmly
environment	9, 19	surroundings
auditory	6	hearing, pertaining to the ear
conscious(ly)	10	aware, knowingly
non-aversive	19	favorable, doesn't turn one away
conducive	19, 22	leading toward

Each word will be discussed in greater detail in Chapter 2, "Break Learning Elements into Manageable Parts." But if you are uncertain about how they are used in sentences, look them up in the paragraphs noted above. Pronunciation guide for these and following terms is on page 16, in the check-up quiz at the end of Chapter 1.

24. Study the following, common psychological terms:

    neurotic: over-anxious, abnormal feelings and emotions

    psychotic: severe mental disorder, out of contact with reality

    obsessive: intense preoccupation of a repetitive nature

    compulsive: extreme drive toward orderly behavior for its own sake

We may all have some kind of neurosis, or neurotic tendencies, at some times in our lives. Psychotic tendencies, or psychoses, are much more serious and need professional treatment.

An obsessive-compulsive performs acts that have little or no usefulness: stacking newspapers in near-perfect order; counting all the boards in a picket fence. One could write:

    His **obsessive-compulsive neuroses** worsened to the point where he became **psychotic** and needed to be hospitalized.

25. Now try the following quiz over these ten psychological terms. Fill in the blanks with words from the list on the right:

1. You can (a) ——————— your learning by
            strengthen

    (b) ——————— using (c) ——— and visual aids.
     being aware   hearing

    Your (d) ——————— can be either (e) ———
         surroundings   leading

    ——— or (f) ——————— to effective learning.
   toward   turned away

2. An (a) ———————————fear of death can
        intense preoccupation

    change one from an (b) ——————— to a
                 over-anxious

    (c) ——————————— state of mind.
   severe mental disorder

aversive
auditory
consciously
compulsive
environment
conducive
neurotic
obsessive
psychotic
reinforce

26. **NOTE:** The study of the "meaning of meaning" is called **semantics**, from the Greek word for "sign." The study of semantics helps us understand that words mean different things to different people—and that our emotions and biases play a strong part in the way we respond to various words.

Check your responses with the answer key on the left-hand page. If you missed any, write the terms and their meaning on the same page. Then read both word and meaning aloud.

26. A word about meanings and some more psychological terms—Here's one caution to keep in mind as you learn new words. Although simple meanings are listed for words in this book, *words do not have meanings in and of themselves.* It's people who put the meanings into words. Several problems arise.

(A) Sometimes people are aware that they have not been using words in precisely the same way. For example, "dope" may include marijuana to some people but not to others. Recognizing this, the speakers need to decide just what the word "dope" is to include in their conversation.

(B) Sometimes people *think* they are using terms in the same way but they are not. A "religious" person might mean "someone who believes in God" to one person but it might mean "someone who believes in the sacredness of life" to another. The speakers need to clearly define what the terms they are using include for each of them. They should not make assumptions about *their* meaning being *everybody's* meaning.

(C) Sometimes people use words and really do not have any clear idea to what they are referring. Some of the words that fall in this category might be: justice, patriotism, love, hate, freedom, duty. These are words that are difficult to define so as to be sure people are communicating. You will learn more about methods of defining words in Chapter 7. But it is important to keep in mind from the start that words can mean different things to different people.

27. Definitions of terms are especially tricky in the field of psychology. When labels are put on people, trouble can arise. A professional labels (or diagnoses) a person; the professional knows that the label is used for a kind of "shorthand" purpose. The label includes some ways in which that person is thinking and acting *at that time.* The last phrase is most important. Patients, like other people, change. They may learn new and better ways of moving around in their worlds; they may learn how to "cope" better with their life roles; they may forget or not use ways they know; or they may get worse. The label that is applied today, even if it has some specific meaning, may not apply tomorrow or next year.

28. **NOTE:** The prefix **para-** is a curious one. Besides the meaning "beyond" as in **paranoid,** it also means:

beside or *alongside of* as in:	*faulty* or *irregular* as in:
parallel	paradox
para-professional	parasite
parable	
parochial	
parody	
paraphrase	

28. This is a very important point to keep in mind when using words. We not only have to be very careful about the meanings we place upon words, but we have to be constantly aware that people and things change and that the words we apply at one time may not fit at another. Take the following four words that are heard frequently in psychology.

> Paranoid
> Schizophrenia (pronounced skitz-o-fren-i-a)
> Introvert
> Extrovert

These terms are frequently misunderstood and misused.

29. Paranoid behaviors take two general forms: distrust and suspicion of others on the one hand and tremendous feeling of self-importance on the other. The term means literally:

para (beyond) **noid** (mind: a Greek word, **nous**, meaning "mind")

30. The term schizophrenia means literally:

schizo (split) **phrenia** (mind)

The schizophrenic has "split" from reality. But there are many kinds of schizophrenia; many schizophrenics can learn to "cope," to handle roles as parents, workers, or students. Some of the fright can be taken out of these terms when their meanings are clarified.

31. The layman, as compared to the professional, may be guilty of labeling someone incorrectly or too harshly. We may call someone "paranoid" because that person thinks that some people do not like him. It may be true that some people do not like him but before we label him "paranoid," we have to check that and other data.

32. The terms **extrovert** and **introvert** are frequently misused. **Vert** comes from a Latin word meaning "turn." **Intro-** means "inside of" and **extro-** means "outside of." So in a very general sense: an **introvert** is "turned inside himself," an **extrovert** is "turned outside himself."

More specifically, an introvert generally refers to one who is apt to handle his feelings inside himself, without discussing them with others. An extrovert is more apt to talk over his feelings, discussing his reactions and emotions with others.

33. If you see a person who is very friendly and talkative in one situation, and a week later you see her sitting alone staring off into space, will you label that person as an introvert or an extrovert? You can't tell. So, we need to be careful about the labels that we fling around. We need to recognize that words do not have meanings; only people do.

34. And so with many words in the area of human behavior. People use terms like "nervous," "upset," "crazy." These are vague terms with little meanings other than what we put into them. Unfortunately, they are sometimes treated as causes, as when someone says: "I can't work because I am so nervous," or "I'm too upset to enjoy anything today." We need to ask the person who makes these kinds of statements what she or he means by "nervous" or "upset." So with the other psychological terms. Does the speaker, or writer, know how she or he is using the word? Is the meaning clear?

35. So we have

> paranoia
> schizophrenia
> introvert
> extrovert

Both paranoia and schizophrenia refer to acute mental disorders, to psychoses rather than neuroses. Introverts and extroverts, on the other hand, are behavioral labels, frequently well within the range of normal behavior. Remember that these are merely labels chosen to have some agreed-upon meanings.

36. So, one of the most important things to remember about meanings of words is that these meanings must be placed within a certain *time*. Take the words

> convict   student   surgeon   parent

You know what they all mean. What they mean to you may not be what they mean to someone else. But as labels, they have to be watched because they can change.

	the convict
can become a	student
who can become a	surgeon
who can become a	parent

Or: A student may be a parent who becomes a surgeon and then becomes a convict. The point is: be careful about thinking of words as having meanings within themselves, unchanging, on-going. No! Words change because people change. Meanings come from people, not from any kind of inner quality within the words!

37. This kind of sophistication about words and their meanings will help you use your growing vocabulary more effectively. And a good vocabulary is one of the more reliable indicators of the successful person. Having a good vocabulary is why one many may move up in the business world while another fails to budge. And that may also be why one woman is looked up to, listened to, while another sinks back in greyness.

Do you wish to review any of the psychological terms or the three word elements (**ex-, dict, voc**) before continuing? When you are ready, turn the page and take the check-up quiz.

Chapter 1: Check-up Quiz

In Chapter 1 you have studied three word elements (**ex-**, **voc**, and **dic** or **dict**) and fourteen psychological terms.

Read the words below *aloud,* paying attention to the pronunciation guide when provided. Then fill in the meanings, referring to paragraphs where words originally occurred *only* if necessary.

A.	Word Elements	Sample Words	Paragraph
	1. **Ex-**	**ex**-officio, **ex**-wife	12
	2. **Voc**	**voc**al, **voc**ation,	
		in**voc**ation	14
	3. **Dic, dict**	**dic**tate, **dic**tator,	
		dictionary	14

Word Element Meaning

1. _____

2. _____

3. _____

B.		Word	Meaning	Paragraph(s)
	1.	reinforce (re-in-**force**)	_____	6, 23
	2.	auditory (**aw**-dih-tor-y)	_____	6, 23
	3.	environment (in-**viron**-ment)	_____	9, 23
	4.	conscious (**con**-shus)	_____	10, 23
	5.	non-aversive (non-uh-ver-siv)	_____	19, 23
	6.	conducive (con-**du**-siv)	_____	19, 22
	7.	neurotic (new-**rah**-tik)	_____	24
	8.	psychotic (sy-**kah**-tik)	_____	24

Word	Meaning	Paragraph(s)
9. obsessive (ob-**ses**-siv)	_____	24
10. compulsive (com-**pul**-siv)	_____	24
11. paranoia (para-**noy**-ya)	_____	29
12. schizophrenia (skitz-o-**fren**-ya)	_____	30
13. introvert (**in**-tro-vert)	_____	32
14. extrovert (**ex**-tro-vert)	_____	32

Check your responses with the following answer key. Once you are sure you have written in appropriate meanings for each term, read the entire list _aloud_ again. Then take the master quiz over the entire chapter from the back-matter.

Chapter 1: Check-up Quiz Completed

A. Word Elements   Meanings

    1. **Ex-:** out of, out, formerly

    2. **Voc:** to call, calling, speech

    3. **Dic, dict:** to speak, words

B.   Word   Meaning

    1. reinforce: to strengthen, implant firmly

    2. auditory: hearing, pertaining to the ear

    3. environment: surroundings

    4. conscious: aware, knowingly

    5. non-aversive: favorable, doesn't turn one away

    6. conducive: leading toward

    7. neurotic: over-anxious, abnormal feelings and emotions

    8. psychotic: severe mental disorder; out of contact with reality

Word	Meaning

9. obsessive: intense preoccupation of a repetitive nature

10. compulsive: an extreme drive toward orderly behavior for its own sake

11. paranoia: distrust of others plus tremendous self-importance; acute mental disorder

12. schizophrenia: a mind split from reality; an acute psychosis or mental disorder

13. introvert: seldom discusses his feelings with others

14. extrovert: frequently discusses his feelings with others

3. **NOTE**: Several prefixes have to do with amounts or numbers.

semi-	half
mono-	one
bi-	two
multi-	many
poly-	many

Can you think of others?

4. **NOTE**: Comprehensible links the word element **com-** to **prehensible.** Do you know what a "prehensile tail" is? It is one that is capable of wrapping around objects, like a monkey's tail.

Chapter 2

Break Learning Elements

into Manageable Parts

1. Learning something about the first ten amendments to the Constitution, more frequently called the "Bill of Rights," or learning the parts of a motorcycle engine can be difficult or fairly simple depending on how you tackle the job. Both are complicated instruments and need to be broken into sections in order to be understood.

2. And so it is with learning words. In Chapter 1, you read:

> Looking up a list of 100 words in the dictionary is not a very effective learning device for most of us . . . but recognizing frequently used prefixes and roots . . . does help.

In the next few chapters you will learn many prefixes and roots which you can recognize in thousands of words—once you begin looking for them. You can break your learning elements (words) into manageable parts (syllables), and thus learn more effectively and efficiently. In the first part of Chapter 2, you will be breaking individual words into manageable parts. In the second part, you will be working with groups of words.

3. You know that many words people have trouble with are words of more than one syllable. Breaking these multi-syllabic words into manageable parts can make them comprehensible. For example, take the words

> multi-syllabic (multi-si-**lab**-ik)
> comprehensible (com-pre-**hen**-si-ble)

You know that **multi** means "many," as in **multi**tude. You know the word **syllable**, so **multi-syllabic** simply means with more than one syllable.

4. And you know that to **comprehend** means "to understand." The last part, -**ible**, means "capable of" so **comprehensible** means "capable of being understood."

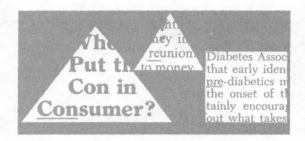

6. **NOTE: A-** is a prefix that you will meet again. For example, the word **amoral** means "outside of morality," neither moral nor immoral. Is science amoral? Scientific research should be largely conducted away from judgments about "good and evil." Do you agree?

Breaking words into syllables can help you: recognize syllables you know—and will learn in this text, spell words, and pronounce words.

5. The prefixes and roots you will learn in these next two chapters are usually just one syllable. Remember **ex-**, the prefix in Chapter 1, and the roots **dict** and **voc?** Each is one syllable. There are exceptions, as in the prefixes **extro-** and **intro-** used in **extrovert** and **introvert.**

6. You can lean heavily on your own ear many times in breaking words into syllables. You probably know more than you realize. For example, consider some of the words in the first chapter:

(A) Pre-bedtime (paragraph 20): Obviously, three syllables: pre-bed-time. Bedtime you know. **Pre-** means "before" as in **pre**-packaged or **pre**-arranged.

(B) Aversive: Again, three syllables: a-ver-sive. **Vers** means "to turn." The first syllable, **a-**, means "away" or "outside of" (pronounce **a-** as "uh" in this word). In Chapter 1, the word non-

aversive was used. What does **non-** mean? _____
(as in **nonsense, non-**redeemable) Not? Correct. So non-aversive behavior means behavior that does *not* turn people away.

7. How many syllables are in some of the other words from Chapter 1? Fill in the blanks:

conducive has _____ syllables

reinforce has _____ syllables

environment has _____ syllables

Did you write: both conducive and reinforce have three syllables and environment has four? Correct.

8. If you break these words into manageable parts, can you recognize word elements in any of the syllables? Take a look at **conducive** (con-duc-ive): **con-** means "with" as in **concave** (*with* a cave), or **conform** (*with* the same form).

Duc comes from **duct**, as in **duct** glands or sewer **ducts**, and it means "to lead."

Reinforce (re-in-force): **re-** means "back" or "again" as in **repeat, re-do.**

N–24

Inforce is spelled differently but means the same as **enforce**, as in law **enforce**ment. So **reinforce** means "to enforce again."

9. You can recognize the following word elements in a variety of words. Fill in the meaning for each, check your answers with the answer key, and then try the check-up quiz that follows:

Meaning		Meaning	
ex- (or e-)	_____	dict (or dic)	_____
con-	_____	voc (or vok)	_____
re-	_____	duc (or duct)	_____

Fill in blank spaces with word elements from list above.

1. Following his in _____ tion into the army, he was _____ vinced
      (lead)   (with)

   that he would be _____ hausted most of the time.
                    (out of)

2. Her _____ ion during the in _____ ation was not _____
       (speech)   (calling)   (with)

   prehensible.

3. I will _____ iterate, or say again: "read words aloud!"
          (again)

Check your responses with the answer key. Be sure your spelling checks with that in the key. Then read aloud the completed words from the answer key.

10. In the fourteen psychological terms you used in Chapter 1 quizzes, nine have word elements at the beginning which are common and thus useful to learn. You will be studying all of them in this text. Just glance over the list now:

Term	begins with	which means
introvert	intro-	inside of
extrovert	extro-	outside of
obsession	ob-	on, against
compulsion	com-	with (same as con-)

10. **NOTE:** Don't confuse these words:

unconsciously, consciously with conscience

The first ones, unconsciously and consciously, have to do with awareness, as in "I was unconscious"—meaning "out of it." Conscience refers to an assumed ability to tell right from wrong, as in "my conscience tells me to do thus-and-so."

12. **NOTE:** For easier comprehension, the roots in this text are spelled in their most common English form. List of Latin and Greek forms is given at the end of the master list of prefixes, roots and suffixes, on **pages 225-228.**

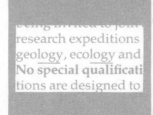

Term	begins with	which means
non-aversive	**non-**	not
	a-	away, outside of
reinforce	**re-**	back, again
environment	**en-**	in, into
conducive	**con-**	with
conscious	**con-**	with

Many words in the chapter have word elements you can spot when you break the words apart. For example:

Term	Word element	Meaning	Used in
neurotic	**neuro**	nerves, nervous system	neuro-surgeon neuron neuritis
psychotic	**psych**	mind, behavior	psychology psychiatrist
auditory	**audit**	hearing, pertaining to the ear	auditorium audit (as in to "audit a course")

11. You know that some of these word elements are called "prefixes" and some are called "roots." Some of the prefixes you have already studied are:

pre-	**re-**	**a-**	**intro-**
ex-, e-	**non-**	**con-**	**extro-**

Some of the roots you have already studied are:

dict	**duc**	**neuro**
voc	**psych**	

You need to be clear on how the terms *roots* and *prefixes* are used.

12. Roots: words or word elements from which other words are formed. The ones you will be studying in this text come primarily from Latin and Greek. Roots usually name things or show some kind of action: **duc**, to lead; **neuro**, nerves or nervous system.

13. **NOTE:** Do not confuse **bi** meaning "two" with **bio** which means "life"—as in **bio**logy or **bio**psy.

Bi- meaning "two" occurs in such words as:

> **bi**-monthly—every two months
> **bi**-motored—having two motors

Have you heard the term serial monogamy? It refers to marriages-in-series. It is a way to retain monogamy, one man married to one woman (at a time). That marriage, then another marriage, then another—with divorces in between!

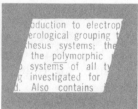

14. **NOTE:** We have many words in English to indicate the process of thinking:

> to think
> to meditate
> to ponder
> to contemplate
> to reflect on
> to ruminate
> to query, to question . . . (sometimes thinking is involved when we ask questions)

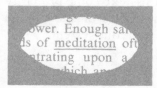

The word **psychology** links two roots:

psych	with	**log**
meaning mind or behavior		meaning the study of

So **psychology** is the study of the mind or, more specifically, of behavior.

13. Prefixes: word elements, often from Latin or Greek, which are added to the front of the roots and which change the meaning, direction or quantity of the root. For example: if you are a **big-amist**, you are married to two or more people at the same time.

If you are a **polygam**ist, you have many wives or husbands.

	Prefix	Root
Bigamy	**bi-** (meaning "two")	
Polygamy	**poly-** (meaning "many")	**gam** (meaning "marriage")

Mono- is a prefix meaning "one." Therefore **monogamy** would be

_____ marriage, or one person married to one other person.

To the eight prefixes listed in paragraph 11, you can now add:

bi meaning _____ as in **bi**cycle, **bi**gamist

mono- meaning _____ as in **mono**cle, **mono**gamist

Notice the pronunciations of

bigamy	**be-guh**-me
monogamy	mo-**naw**-guh-me

14. The word **prefix** has the prefix _____ in it, which means

_____ .

What do you suppose Pre-history means? Before history? Well, not quite. It actually refers to things that happened *before* records were kept, before recorded history. Pre-historic Man, then, refers to early man, about 7000 years ago. Before that time we had nothing recorded, written down about man; thus, we call the time before 5000 B.C. "Pre-history."

You may have heard of pre-meditated murders. Do you know what

"meditation" is? _____ . Did you write "thinking?" Right. So pre-meditation means thinking out the murder beforehand, planning it in advance. Now, add the prefix **pre-** to the following roots and see what you come up with:

_____ gnant

_____ judice

_____ position

15. As suggested in Chapter 1, read the words *aloud* before going on; use as many of the senses as possible in order to learn efficiently.

    The first one, pregnant, refers to a time "before birth." Some authorities say that the root comes from **nasci-**, which means "to be born." You can think of prejudice as being "before knowledge or judgment." And prepositions are those little words that may have given you trouble: by, in, through, around, under, over. For example, *by* you, *in* fact, *through* me, *around* him, *under* it, *over* the wall.

16. Using just these prefixes:

    bi-, mono- (or **mon-**), and **pre-**

    Try this short quiz. Fill in blanks with one of the prefixes:

    1. A stamp that is cancelled *before* mailing is called a _____ cancelled stamp.

    2. A report that was written once every *two* years would be a

       _____ annual report. (If a report comes out twice a year, for a six-month period, it is called a **semi**-annual—or half-year—report. So **semi** means _____ . Right! **Semi-** means "half.")

    3. You may have played the game in which *one* person sometimes

       gets all the property; the game is called _____ poly. (**Poly** in this case comes from the Greek word meaning "to sell"; it does not come from the word meaning "many," as you may have thought.)

18. **NOTE:** You can form many, many words by linking these common prefixes with other word elements. Usually a hyphen is not used:

extract	substantial
nonverbal	transient
automatic	

In some cases, a hyphen may be used: (1) when the word element following the prefix begins with a capital:

ex-Cuban	trans-Canadian
non-French	

(2) when the hyphen is necessary to clarify meaning:

ex-nun
trans-sexual

nvestigative tool
subpoenas, subpo
he threat of cont
sses are reluctant
ht be subpoena
e prosecutor, son

at transportation costs
art of education budg
at only a minute porti
in transportation costs

that the autho
was afraid to trust
nonprofessional

Answer Key

18. graph: monograph, autograph
plane: mono-plane (1 set of wings)
bi-plane (2 sets of wings)
husband: ex-husband
historic: prehistoric
non-historic
sequential: non-sequential
consequential
plan: preplan
replan
fine: confine
refine
way: subway

4. An idea that is conceived *before*hand is called a_____con-
ceived idea.

5. The word partisan comes from the same root as the word party
and participation; partisan means "interested in one cause or
party." A committee that has *two* parties (political parties,

that usually means) could be called _____partisan.

6. One ruler, a king or queen, for example, is called a _____ -
arch. (Arch means "chief" or "ruler.")

17. Check yourself with answer key at bottom of page N-30; make
corrections as needed. Write at least two words beginning with **pre-,**
mono-, bi-. You may wish to check these words with your dictionary or your instructor.

Record words you spot which use these **prefixes—pre-, mono-,**
bi-

18. Now try four more prefixes which you may know but not *know*
you know.

non-, auto-, trans-, sub-

(A) You know that **non-** means "not" as in **non-**aversive, or **non-**
sense. Now link it with

sequitur (meaning   to make _____ sequitur (meaning not
sequence or order)   in sequence or order)

involvement   to make _____ -involvement

productive   to make _____- _____

(B) An automobile is mobilized by one's self. So **auto** means "self."

If you can regulate yourself, you have _____ nomy. Did you
write autonomy? Right. You are autonomous. You can do it
yourself.

(C) **Trans-** is another easy one. TWA, Trans World Airlines, means
"across" the world. Transfer is across, from one line to another.
Trans means "across." A **trans**ient is one who moves around or
across the country.

(D) Another useful and commonly seen prefix is **sub-.** You know
that a **sub**way is a way "under"—or a method of travel that takes

you underground. But do you know what a subpoena is? Well, **poena** comes from the word meaning "penalty." So, if you get a subpoena, you are *under penalty* to appear in court.

Do you know what subordinate means? You know the word "order." **Sub**ordinate means "*under* someone's order, lower in rank." In the army, a colonel is **sub**ordinate to a general; an enlisted man is **sub**ordinate to an officer. Subnormal means *below* average or *below* normal, and **sub**oceanic means *under* the ocean. Then there's **sub**marine, **sub**standard, **sub**total and **sub**vocal.

You now have eleven simple, useful prefixes to aid you in learning new words. Fill in the meanings for each of them below, referring to the paragraphs noted *only* when necessary. Then link as many prefixes as you can to the words on the right. Note that in some cases more than one prefix can be added to the words on the right, as in first example.

Prefix	Meaning	Used in Paragraph	add as many prefixes as you can to these words
Ex-	_____	12 (Ch. 1)	scribe prescribe, transcribe subscribe
Pre-	_____	6, 14 (Ch. 2)	graph _____
A-	_____	6	plane _____
Non-	_____	6, 18	husband _____
Con-	_____	8	historic _____
Re-	_____	8	sequential _____
Bi-	_____	13	plan _____
Mono-	_____	13	fine _____
Auto-	_____	18	way _____
Trans-	_____	18	
Sub-	_____	18	

Did you include the following:

(A) Your **autograph** is your signature—written by your*self*.

(B) If you **refine** something, you work it over *again*, to make improvements; if you **confine** something, you keep it *with*in, or imprison it.

(C) A **monograph** is a book or pamphlet on *one* subject.

(Check your responses with the answer key found on page N–32.)

19. In this text, you will be learning *parts* of words besides the prefixes and roots in this chapter. You will be an expert at word analysis, on breaking words apart and understanding how to use them.

20. Another way to break learning vocabulary into manageable parts is to study a small group of words about a related topic. Any topic will do—words on engines, on French cooking, insurance terms, or words used in soccer. Don't try to learn too many at once, at least not at the beginning. You know best how much *you* can manage.

21. Let's say you take out liability insurance on a car or bike. You read over the policy and see several terms you are not quite certain about, such as:

> premium   limits of liability
>
> inception date   deductible clause
>
> expiration date

You note that four out of five terms use prefixes; all but **de-** in deductible you already have studied. But some of the words seem to have a special meaning in this policy: (Fill in blanks as you go along.)

1. Premium: You know that "to set a high premium on something" means to give it a high value. But the premium on an insurance policy simply means the amount you pay for that policy, for the privilege of being insured. The premium can be

   paid on an annual (yearly), a semi-annual (_____ -yearly), quarterly, or monthly basis.

2. The inception and expiration dates you can figure out: inception is when the policy goes *into* effect and expiration is when

   it goes _____ , or expires.
   ex-

Answer Key
21. 1. half
2. out
3. liable
4. to lead
1. c
2. b
3. e
4. a
5. d

3. Limits of liability simply means the limit of responsibility, or how far the insurance company will go in paying for any accident. Liability insurance is required in many states. If you are responsible for an accident or damage to person or property,

   you are held _____ .

4. Deductibility clause: **de-** is a prefix meaning "down" or "away." You will read more on that later. **Duct**, you know,

   means _____ . So deduct means "to lead or take away." You will have to pay part of the cost yourself if you have a deductible clause—often $50 or $100. It's a good thing to know about.

Check your fill-ins above with answer key.

Now match the terms on the left with the meanings on the right.

1. _____ premium   a. how much the company will
                                        pay
2. _____ inception date
                                     b. when policy begins
3. _____ expiration date   c. amount policy costs
                                     d. how much you have to pay
4. _____ limits of liability   if you have an accident
5. _____ deductible clause   e. when policy ends.

Check your responses with answer key.

22. Finally, other terms appearing on insurance policies that you may want to look up are such as: waiver, beneficiary, subrogation, dividend. If you have an insurance policy, take it out and look up other words that are unfamiliar to you. Remember to learn them in small—or manageable—groups. Taking on a few at a time is a wise Learning Technique.

23. If you are not very familiar with engines, you may want to learn the simplified meanings for the small group of words in the following chart. If you are familiar with engines, you may still want to pay special attention to the column on the right. It may not have occurred to you how many of the terms about engines are used in other ways.

    As with the terms on your insurance policy, several of these terms on engines begin with prefixes that you know: **trans**mission, **ex**haust, even **sus**pension (a form of the prefix **sub-**).

Answer Key

25. 1. translated
   autobiography
   monotone
   2. pre-packaged
   substitute
   3. mono-plane
   bi-plane
   non-combatant
   4. conversation
   referred
   exorbitant

Term	Meaning	How else used
Transmission	carries—or transmits—power from crank shaft to drive shaft	Trans- TWA or Trans World Airlines trans-Atlantis transistor mission (or "send") missionary missile
Generator	creates—or generates—electrical current for engine	"This text will **generate** interest in word study."
Distributor	sends—or distributes—electricity to all spark plugs	"I will **distribute** the money." "This **distribution** center is closed."
Exhaust pipe	releases waste material from engine	"You have made an **exhaustive** study of the problem."
Manifold	multiple pipes going to a common outlet	"Many (mani-) are folding into one."
Suspension system	springs and shock absorbers to withstand road wear	"Keep me in **suspense**."

24. There is no check-up quiz on the insurance or engine terms above. They are given here for two reasons:

    1. to help you learn words by grouping them into manageable units;

    2. to help you identify word elements you know as you break words apart into syllables.

25. But before you take the master quiz in the back matter over the rest of the chapter, review the prefixes and their meanings in paragraph 18. Then take the following check-up quiz.

    1. He _____ lated the _____ biography in a _____ tone.
           (across)   (self)   (one)

    2. A _____ -packaged meal will _____ stitute when time is at a
          (before)   (under)
       premium.

3. I prefer a _____ plane to a _____ plane for _____-combatant fly-
          (one)   (two)   (not)
   ing.

4. His _____ versation _____ ferred totally to the _____ orbitant
      (with)   (back)   (out of)
   prices at the fair.

NOTE: The prefix **a-** is not used at all; the prefix **mono-** is used twice. Check your responses with the answer key. Then try the second part of this check-up quiz, again using words in context.

Chapters 1, 2: Check-up Quiz

Read the following passage. In the blank spaces fill in the prefix or root that best fits the meaning given below the blank. In some instances, the prefix and roots are combined. When you are finished, read the following completed passage; make any corrections on your fill-ins that are necessary.

P _____ studies show that your _____ can
  (mind)   (study of)   (surroundings)

____inforce your learning. But it must be____ducive to gaining knowl-
(again)   (with)

edge. Only you can____vert it to your learning style. If you have a
              (with)

_____ disposition toward learning new words, you won't find the task
(before)

_____cessively difficult. However, if learning new words is _____
(out of)   (turned away)

to you, if it is not high on your list of priorities, you may have limited success. Your personal goals must include word study.

Constant word analysis is vital. Use _____and visual
                                (hearing)

aids. Break words into word elements: roots and affixes, including

_____ fixes and _____fixes. Studying a list of twenty or 100 new
 (before)   (under or after)

words is often _____ tonous and _____ productive. But learning a
          (one)   (not)

few word elements at a time and applying them to dozens of other words *can* be your gateway to greater word power.

NOTE: Kinetic has the same root as cinema—both dealing with "motion." Kinetic energy is energy in motion; the cinema is made up of pictures in motion.

Chapters 1, 2: Check-up Quiz Completed

Psychological studies show that your environment can reinforce your learning. But it must be conducive to gaining knowledge. Only you can convert it to your learning style. If you have a predisposition toward learning new words, you won't find the task excessively difficult. However, if learning new words is aversive to you, if it is not high on your list of priorities, you may have limited success. Your personal goals must include word study.

Constant word analysis is vital. Use auditory and visual aids. Break words into word elements: roots and affixes, including prefixes and suffixes. Studying a list of twenty or 100 words is often monotonous and nonproductive. But learning a few word elements at a time and applying them to dozens of other words *can* be your gateway to greater word power.

Did you fill in all thirteen blanks correctly? Excellent. Then you are probably ready for the tear-out quiz over Chapter 2. You may wish to review the roots and prefixes listed at the end of paragraph 18. Keep in mind that jotting down notes on the left-hand pages can aid your learning. The more of your senses—auditory, visual, motion (kinetic)—you use the better.

When you are ready, take the master-quiz over this chapter that appears in the back of the book.

Chapter 3

Link the Unknown

to the Known

1. When you learn, you link new ideas, or knowledge of things, to what you already know. That is much of what learning is all about. Often you form these links unconsciously, without being aware of what is going on.

2. But you can also *consciously* link the unknown to the known. For example, you can link prefixes you have learned to roots you don't know but are learning. You can put them together so that you add hundreds, even thousands, of words to your vocabulary.

3. In this chapter you will link prefixes you have learned to new roots. You will also learn some new prefixes. The first roots you will deal with are **vert** and **mitt**.

   Vert: the root in aversive. It is written both as **vert** and **vers**. We no longer use the word **vert** by itself. If you said to someone:

   "Vert left at the next corner,"

   chances are that person would not understand you. Yet you use many **vers**ions of the word.

4. You know that aversive means "to turn away," **a-** meaning "away," and **vers** (or **vert**) meaning _____ . By adding various prefixes to the root **vert**, you can build a whole wheel of words:

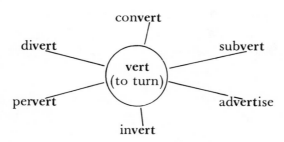

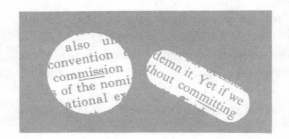

5. You can do the same thing with **vers**:

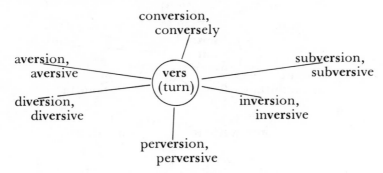

6. NOTE: On the word wheels, when words are used that have been analyzed previously, such as aversive, or that are well-known, such as advertise, no further treatment will be given. When further treatment is given, you may wish to fill in meanings on the word wheels.

7. You know that to convert someone, to perform a conversion, is to "turn someone *with* you," to make a **convert** out of him. But conversely means "turned around" or "reversed."

8. To divert someone's attention is to "turn it away," to create a diversion. To invert is to "turn it within"; to subvert is "to turn it under"; to pervert is to "turn completely" or to corrupt.

9. **Mitt**: the root in remittance, mission. Like **vert**, it has two common forms: **mitt (mit)** and **miss**. A mission is a place to which people are sent. They are often called "missionaries." A missile is a kind of

   rocket that is _____ into space. So **mitt** or **miss** means "to send." We also have

   Transmit—send across
   Remit—send back
   Intermittent—to send periodically, between other things.

10. Following is a word wheel with the root **mitt** (or **mit**). Note when the second *t* is dropped.

   You use two *t*'s when the syllable following the root **mitt** begins with a vowel, as in admittance, intermittent. Otherwise, you use only one *t*: submit, omit, emit.

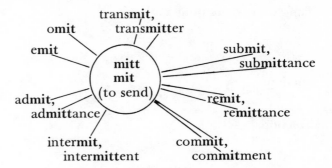

11. You can make a similar wheel using **mission**. Fill in as many of the blanks as you can, referring to prefixes above for guides.

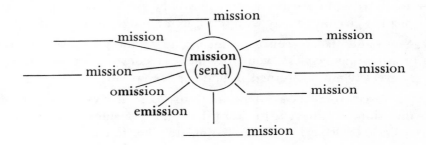

12. Emission, you are probably familiar with. If your exhaust emission is blue, you are burning too much oil. To emit is to "send out." Do you know the word emissary, one who is sent out? As in an emissary of good will, or an ambassador.

13. Notice that commit and commission both have two *m*'s: prefix **com-** plus root **mitt** or **miss**.

14. Remember that **vert** or **vers** means _____ and **mitt** or **miss** means _____ .

15. The next two roots are easy ones: **spect** and **scribe**. Both you have seen before, as in:

Spect	Scribe
spectacles	scribble
spectators	inscription
inspect	describe

One means "to look," the other "to write." Which is which: **spect**:

_____ **scribe**: _____ .

16. **Spect**: the root in inspect, inspector. Spectator sports are ones where more people look on rather than play, right? Fishing is generally not thought of as a spectator sport; basketball frequently is.

17. **Scribe**: The root in scribble, scriptures. You will recall that scribes copy things. You can picture them sitting on high stools with dim candles laboring over old manuscripts and carefully copying the words.

18. You may wish to draw your own word wheels on the next left-hand page for **spect** and **scribe**. Besides the words above, you could add:

Spect	**Scribe**
introspection (to look inside)	prescription
spectacular	scriptures (sacred writings)
specter (ghost)	script (handwriting, also the text of a play)
circumspect (to look around, be cautious)	

19. **Circum-** can be added to both **spect** and **scribe**. It is a prefix meaning "around," as to circumnavigate the globe, or sail around it. Circumspect behavior is very careful, prudent behavior; to circumscribe something is to draw a line around it, to enclose it.

20. Now match the roots on the left with the appropriate meanings on the right by filling in the blanks with the meanings; then write a sample word in the column on the far right.

Root	Meaning (choose one)	Sample Word
1. **vert, vers** _____	A. to send	_____
2. **mitt, miss** _____	B. to look	_____
3. **scribe** _____	C. to turn	_____
4. **spect** _____	D. to write	_____
5. **duc, duct** _____	E. to lead	_____

21. And when you get fancier changes on these—with letters changed and suffixes added at the end, you can figure out what they mean by linking the unknown to the known. Write down what you think the following terms mean.

20. List as many other words as you can think of using these roots:

vert, vers	mitt, miss	scribe	spect	duc, duct
Sample: convert	admit	prescribe	inspect	conduct

For Western
book. The ge
logistics are b
a military sp
ogy is not eas
keeps shifting

ronic intel
on, for his up-
a psychological
sexual buffoon,
tern world fo
s as

d offe
rocess in train
circumstances
their c

Answer Key

20. 1. vert, vers: to turn
    2. mitt, miss: to send
    3. scribe: to write
    4. spect: to look
    5. duc, duct: to lead

Check preceding pages *and* your dictionary for sample words.

Term	Meaning
1. King James Version	_____
2. Inter-Continental Ballistics Missiles (ICBM)	_____
3. Retranscribe	_____
4. Retrospection	_____
5. Abduct	_____

22. You may not be sure what **retro-** means, but you can probably guess it means the same as **re-**. And you may not be familiar with the prefix **ab-** which means "away" in this usage (as in **ab**normal, **ab**sent). Now you should be able to fill in the meanings of the five terms above. Check your meanings with the ones below:

   1. King James I lived in England in the early 1600s, at a time when the colonization of Jamestown was just beginning in the United States. In King James' court a translation of the Christian Bible was being prepared. It was a new "turning" or version, different from some of the earlier translations in Greek, Latin, French or English.

   2. Missiles are "sent" into space. Some can be sent between continents; they are inter-continental ballistic missiles—or ICBMs.

   3. Transcribing something means to "write it across" from one language or form to another. To retranscribe could mean to do it over again because there were errors in the earlier translation.

   4. If **retro-** means "back" or "again" and **spect** means "to look," then retrospection means "to look back," to think about the past.

   5. To abduct someone is "to lead that person away."

23. It is possible, of course, to make word wheels using prefixes as the center or hub. Just consult your dictionary. But you must be careful. For example, you can use the prefix **ab-** as the hub.

24. But such words as abide, ability, and abdomen (stomach) do not use the prefix **ab-**, so they should *not* appear on the following word wheel.

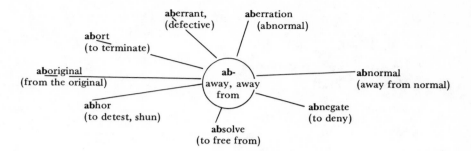

25. Besides building word wheels, another way to link the unknown to the known is to build word pyramids, starting from the top.

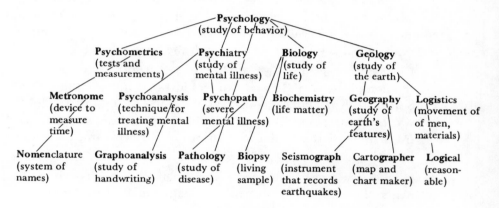

26. Or take a word like premonition, having the prefix **pre-** and the root **mon**, meaning "to warn." If you have a premonition (pre-mo-ni-tion) about something, you have a feeling in advance that it is going to happen. A pyramid starting with premonition could take this shape.

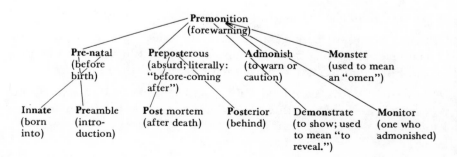

27. Before learning more prefixes and roots, read over the following review of the major prefixes and roots given so far.

Prefixes	Meaning	Roots	Meaning
Ab-	away, away from	**Scrib**	to write
Retro-	back, again	**Spect**	to look
Circum-	around	**Vers, vert**	to turn
E-, ex-	out, formerly	**Mitt, miss**	to send
Pre-	before	**Nasci**	to be born
Non-	not	**Gam (gamy)**	marriage
Con-	with	**Log (logy)**	to study
Re-	back, again	**Neuro**	nerve
Bi-	two	**Psych**	mind, behavior
Mono-		**Duc**	to lead
Mon-	one	**Dict, dic**	to speak
Auto-	self	**Voc**	to call
Trans-	across		
Sub-	under		

28. Take a few minutes to cover up the meanings of the prefixes and say the meaning aloud on each one. Then slide the paper down and check your response. Do the same on the roots. Circle any you missed; then say them aloud several times, thinking of words that use the word element you missed. Try to link it with words you know. For example, if you missed **con-**, meaning "with," try **con**necting it with something you know. Get the **con**nection?

29. Are you familiar with the prefixes **de-** and **dis-**? Can you think of any words that use them? Write down at least two examples of words using each prefix:

    de-   1. _____   2. _____

    dis-   1. _____   2. _____

30. How about some of the roots you just reviewed. Can you add **de-** or **dis-** to any of them? Sure.

        de + scrib = describe meaning to put *down* in words

        de + duct = deduct meaning to lead *down* from

        dis + miss = dismiss meaning to send *away*

And if you drop the *s* from **dis-**, leaving **di-**, you can make:

$$di + vert = divert \text{ meaning to turn } away$$

So **de-** seems to mean _____ , and **dis-** or **di-** seems to

mean _____ .

31. **Caution!** **Di-** also means "two," the same as **bi-**. We do not use it often, but it does appear in dilemma, dioxide and in some other words. More often **di-** means "down" or "away" as in

   Divulge meaning to give away to the people.

   Vulge means "people." The word vulgar comes from the same root! Check your dictionary for the list of words that begin with **de-, di-,** and **dis-**. You will be amazed; there are several pages in desk-size dictionaries for words starting with each one of these prefixes. Some of the ones you will come across are:

De-	Dis-	Di-
detach	displace	divulge
detain	displease	diverse
defrock	dispassionate	diminish
dethrone	dismount	divorce
define	dissect	
de-personalized	disfigure	

32. **De-** generally means "down" or "away." **Dis-** or **di-** generally means "not" or "away." Both suggest negation.

33. You have had four roots so far in this chapter.

spect	vert, vers
scrib	mitt, miss

   Now try three more—**cap** or **cep**, **ject**, and **press**.

34. **Cap:** the root in capture, capable. It takes many forms— **cep, cept, cip, ceive.** Many of the words are well-known, and it is not difficult to figure out how they came from the root **cap** meaning "to take" or "seize."

   Conception is to "take with"; deception is to "take away." Conception refers to pregnancy; deception refers to faking something. Interception you know as something that "goes between"; inception means "the beginning."

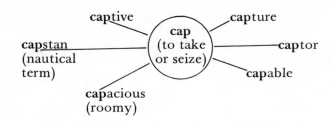

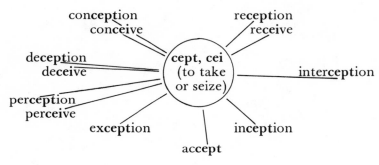

35. **Ject**: the root in projection, inject. It doesn't take as many forms as **cap**, and it is easier to spot. Projection is an important psychological term; if you try to pretend that your wishes, needs, or desires are really the feelings of someone else, you are projecting. **Ject** means "to throw."

36. As with words using **cap**, many words using **ject** are well-known: are you familiar with the self-propelling missiles called projectiles?

37. Many nouns and verbs using **ject** are the same except for the pronunciation. For example:

> I ob**ject** to that **object**.
> His **subjects** were sub**ject**ed to cruelties.

Can you put the following into sentences:

Noun	Verb
project	pro**ject**
reject	re**ject**
deject	de**ject**

38. Other words using **ject** are eject, meaning "to throw _____";

inject, injection, "to throw _____"; abject, "to throw _____ or to be miserable."

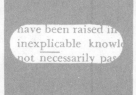

39. **Press**: the root in depression, impress. **Press** is the easiest of the three, because unlike the others, we use it by itself. Choosing either **press** or the synonym **push**, fill in the following blanks:

Example:	Depression:	to push down
	Impression:	_____
	Repress:	_____
	Express:	_____
	Suppress: (prefix **sub-**)	_____

40. You get a spelling aid here again: **suppress** has two *p*'s since the prefix **sup-** is linked to the root **press**. The same is true in oppress. The prefix **op-** (usually written **ob-**) means "against." Oppressive behavior "pushes against us"; it is difficult to bear.

41. Brief review. **Cap** means (a) _____ ; **ject** means (b) _____ ; **press** means (c) _____ .
    Check your responses with the answer key.

42. The last three roots to study in this chapter all begin with *p*: **port**, **pli** or **plic**, and **pon** or **pos**.

43. **Port**: the root in portable, transport. This one is easy: **port** means "to carry." Import: "to carry in." Export: "to carry out."

44. **Pli, plic**: the root in pliable, also in plywood. **Pli** or **plic** means "to fold." Supplicate: "to fold yourself under" (or bow down).

45. **Pon, pos**: the root in component, expose. It means "to put or place." Components are parts *put together;* to expose someone is to *put* him *out* into the open.

46. Now, using the following prefixes, form your own word wheels using the roots **port**, **pli** and **pon** as shown in the hubs on page 58.

Prefixes and Meanings

Dis-: not, away	**E-, ex-**: out, formerly	**Con-, com-**: with
De-: down, away	**Pre-**: before	**Re-**: back, again
Ad-, ap-: to, towards	**Non-**: not	**Sub-, sup-**: under
Ob-, op-: against	**In-, im-**: in, into	**Trans-**: across

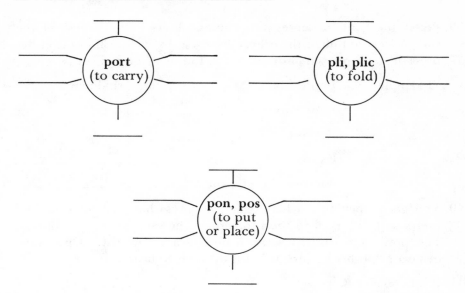

Check your word wheels with the completed ones on pages 58 and 59.

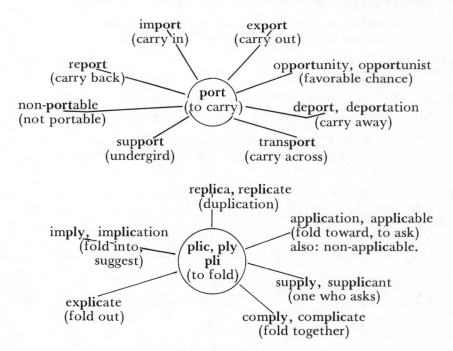

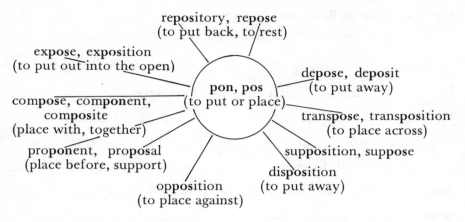

repository, repose
(to put back, to rest)

expose, exposition
(to put out into the open)

depose, deposit
(to put away)

compose, component,
composite
(place with, together)

pon, pos
(to put or place)

transpose, transposition
(to place across)

proponent, proposal
(place before, support)

supposition, suppose

disposition
(to put away)

opposition
(to place against)

47. Some of the words formed have been in our language such a long time that their earlier meanings have shifted: support (to **carry** under); supply (to **fold** under); suppose (to **place** under). Don't worry when these common words have moved away from their earlier meanings. It is the *un*common words you are after.

Check-up Quiz on Roots and Prefixes

Fill in the blanks with the missing prefix, root, or meaning.

Prefixes	Meaning		Roots	Meaning
Pre-	_____		Vert, vers	_____
Mono-	_____		____, ____	to send
_____	two		_____	to write
_____	out of, formerly		Spect	_____
Non-	_____		Duc, duct	_____
Auto-	_____		_____	to carry
_____	across		Pon, pos	_____
_____	under		Plic	_____
Retro-	_____		Voc	_____
Ab-	_____		Dict	_____
_____	down, away		_____	to take or seize
Dis-, di-	_____		_____	to throw
Ob-	_____		Press	_____
Con-	_____		Log (logy)	_____
_____	back, again			
Circum-	_____			

Check your list with the following list. Correct any that need correcting. Read the words and the meanings *aloud*. Then take the master quiz at the back of the book.

Check-up Quiz on Roots and Prefixes Completed

Prefixes	Meaning	Roots	Meaning
Pre-	before	**Vert, vert**	to turn
Mono-	one	**Mitt (mit), miss**	to send
Bi-	two	**Scrib**	to write
Ex-, e-	out of, formerly	**Spect**	to look
Non-	not	**Duc, duct**	to lead
Auto-	self	**Port**	to carry
Trans-	across	**Pon, pos**	to put, place
Sub-	under	**Plic**	to fold
Retro-	back, again	**Voc**	to call
Ab-	away, away from	**Dict**	to speak
De-	down, away	**Cap**	to take, seize
Dis-, di-	not, away	**Ject**	to throw
Ob-	against	**Press**	to push
Con-	with	**Log (logy)**	to study
Re-	back, again		
Circum-	around		

The above list includes the major word elements presented thus far in the text, with the exception of:

Nasci: to be born (as in **r**en**a**issance, **n**a**t**al, innate)
Gam: marriage (as in mono**gam**y, bi**gam**y, poly**gam**y)
Neuro: nerves (as in **neuro**logy, **neuro**-surgeon)
Psych: mind, behavior (as in **psych**ology, **psych**iatrist)

You have over 30 word elements so far from which you can make hundreds of words.

1. **NOTE:** The term **feedback** has come into wide usage with computers. You can get both **negative feedback** and **positive feedback:** information you don't want to hear and information you do want to hear.

4. **NOTE:** Did you read the note on paragraph 12, Chapter 1, asking if you thought scientific research should be **amoral? Amoral** is *not* the same as **immoral. Immorality** assumes an existence of some kind of morality, or "rightness and wrongness." **Amorality** is *outside of* that kind of judgment. It operates apart from moral judgments.

Chapter 4

Get Immediate Feedback

1. If you ask someone a question, you generally want an answer. You want feedback from that person as to whether or not you are correct, or even on the right track. Or you want data from that person to satisfy your question. And it is helpful if you can get that feedback promptly!

2. The same thing is true with the learning that goes on inside your own head. You need to get the nod that what you are learning is what you are supposed to be learning.

3. In order to use the techniques discussed in Chapters 1, 2 and 3, you need to know immediately that you are right on the meanings of specific affixes and roots. Otherwise, you may be timid about using your new-found knowledge. You may not be able to link the unknown to the known unless you are *sure* of your knowns.

4. For example, remember the word aversive in Chapter 1? You may remember that the root **vers** means "turn," because it was used repeatedly.

divert	subvert
convert	pervert
invert	advertise

Only the *s* was changed to a *t*: **vers** to **vert**. But do you remember what the prefix **a-** means? Perhaps not. So when you see:

a-typical	atheist
a-social	amoral

You may not recognize the prefix **a-** as being the same prefix you saw in "aversive." Remember that

    a- means "away from" or "outside of"

so then you can figure out that a-social means (a) _____

_____ ; a-typical means (b) _____ ;

7. **NOTE:** The word reinforce links **re-** with enforce—or, as it is spelled here, inforce. The **in-** from Latin became **en-** in French, as in law **en**forcement. Many other words that come from French use the **en-** spelling: engage, endoctrinate, enjoy, enlightenment, enlist, enslave, envelope—and so on. If you write enforcement, you use the **en-,** but if you write reinforcement, you use the **in-** (**reen**forcement wouldn't work too well, would it!) Checking your dictionary is the safest way to be sure of spelling.

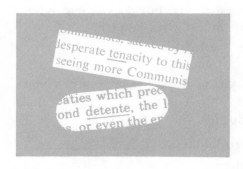

Answer Key

(a) a-social: outside of society
(b) a-typical: not typical
(c) amoral: outside of morality
(d) atheist: away from God
(e) **re:** back
(f) **re:** again
(g) **ten:** to hold
(h) **de:** down
(i) **de:** away
(j) detente: away from tension

amoral means (c) _____ ; atheist (theist means believer in God. "Theos" is the Greek word for God). So an atheist is one who is (d) _____.

But you want to be sure of the meaning of **a-** before you link it to other words.

5. When you run into the phrase "Data **Re**tention Card" in this chapter, you will recognize that the **re-** means (e) _____ or (f) _____, but you may not be sure about the **ten.** You probably know that **detention** means "to hold someone or something down"; you have already studied the prefix **de-** meaning "down" or "away from." So you can figure out that **ten** means (g) _____ _____ .

Retention: holding something for use again and again.

Detention: holding something or someone down.

6. But when you run into the French word detente in the newspapers, as in: "There is an increasing detente between China and the United States" you will want to be sure to remember that **de-** means *both* "down" and "away from." Because **detente** means a "moving away from tension"; it does *not* mean a "holding down." You might misread the sentence if you did not remember that **de-** means both (h) _____ and (i) _____ , and therefore be able to figure out that detente meant (j) _____ _____ .

Check your answers in blanks above with answer key at bottom of left-hand page.

7. Another example: Remember the word reinforce in Chapter 1? You read that the word means "to strengthen" or "repeat." You already know that the prefix **re-** means (a) _____ or (b) _____ _____ as in

> **re**peat
> **re**cover
> **re**set

7. **NOTE:** Two other words using the root **gnos** are:

Diagnostic—**dia-** meaning through
Prognosis—**pro-** meaning before

Both terms are used in the health field: diagnostic or diagnosis meaning "to know through the symptoms" and prognosis meaning "to predict" the outcome of a disease.

You know that re**cogn**ize means to *know* something or someone *again;* so **cogn**ize must have something to do with knowledge. The part **cogn** comes from the word **gnoscere** meaning "to know." Therefore, when you see these words: **cognition** and **cognitive,** you

know they have to do with (c) _____ .

The **gnos** part is used in other words. You know that **gnos** has

something to do with knowledge and that **a-** means (d) _____

_____ , so the word **agnostic** means (e) _____

_____—or specifically, outside of knowledge about God—one who simply does not know whether or not a God exists.

Check your answers in blanks above with answer key at bottom of left-hand page.

8. When you link new parts (unknowns) to old ones (knowns) you have to be *sure* your knowns are correct,

Prefixes	**a-**	"outside of"
	de-	"down" or "away from"
Roots	**ten**	"to hold"
	cogn	"to know"

before you can link them effectively with word elements you are not certain about.

9. You know the learning techniques:

(A) Examine the words in context.

(B) Break the words into manageable parts.

(C) Link the unknown to what you already know.

(D) Get *immediate feedback* on the correctness of your response.

10. You will have hundreds of word elements in this book alone. How on earth can you retain (remember) all of them? How can you be sure you are correct? How can you find out immediately? There is a simple, efficient way to remember various bits of data without spending a great deal of time. You can study most any time or place, and you can go over data easily until you have it down pat. You can avoid going back over things you already know, and you can emphasize work on things you don't know. Here's what you do. You make

Data Retention Cards (DRC)

12. **NOTE:** Can you figure out the difference between an emigrant and an immigrant?

E- or **ex-** means "outside of"

Im- on **in-** means "into" or "within"

So an emigrant is one who *leaves* a country, who goes outside, and an immigrant is one who migrates *to* a country, or comes in.

11. You can break most words into manageable parts called syllables; many words you can break into affixes and roots. Aversive and recognize each have three parts.

Prefix	Root	Suffix
a-	vers	-ive
re-	cogn	-ize

NOTE: a hyphen *follows* prefixes as in (**a-**) and **precedes** suffixes as in (**-ive**). Use no hyphen around roots.

An excellent way to learn these word elements efficiently is to place the elements (prefixes, roots and suffixes) on separate *Data Retention Cards* (DRCs).

12. Data Retention Cards are simply small cards on which you write information you wish to **retain**. Here is the technique:

1. Purchase a package of 3 x 5 index cards.
2. On one side of the card, write, for example, the prefix **ad-**.
3. On the other side of the card, write "to, towards" which is what **ad-** means. Below that, write a sample word you know which uses **ad-** meaning "to" (**adhesive, advance, admission** . . .)

It's as simple as 1-2-3. Your card should look like this:

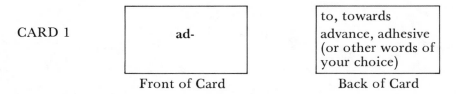

CARD 1 | ad- | to, towards / advance, adhesive / (or other words of / your choice)

Front of Card   Back of Card

Now make up two other Data Retention Cards using the prefixes **a-** and **re-**.

On front of card put: On back of card put:

CARD 2   **A-**   away, outside of
                                 amoral, atheist . . .   DRC
                                                                 a-

CARD 3   **Re-**   back, again
                                 repeat, reset . . .   DRC
                                                                 re-

Now, test yourself on the following prefixes that have been defined earlier in the text. Give the meaning for each prefix you know; then record a word which uses the prefix.

Answer Key

12. pre- before prefix
bi- two bigamy
mono- one monogamy
ad- to, toward advance
auto- self automobile
trans- across Trans-World
sub- under submarine
ex- out of ex-convict
non- not nonsense
poly- many polywogs

Prefix	Meaning	Word Using Prefix	DRC
pre-			pre-
bi-			bi-
mono-			mono-
ad-			ad-
auto-			auto-
trans-			trans-
sub-			sub-
ex-			ex-
non-			non-
poly-			poly-

Check your answers with answer key at bottom of left-hand page. Did you miss any? If so, stop right now and make up DRCs for that prefix. If you missed **bi-** for example, make up a card.

Front of card	Back of card
bi-	two
	bicycle, bigamy

13. Be sure to put the meaning *and* an example on the back side of the card. Use for an example a word you *know* (link the unknown to the known).

14. When you have made up cards for the prefixes, test yourself.

 A. Look at the prefix on the front of card.
 B. Say *aloud* the meaning if you know it—and the sample word or words in which the prefix is used.
 C. *Then* look at the back of the card and check yourself.
 D. If you missed the meaning, put the card at the bottom of your stack. You will test yourself again over that prefix when you reach the bottom. If you miss it a second time, say it aloud several times, trying to think of additional words that use that prefix. You may wish to consult your dictionary, writing down additional sample words on the back of the card.

E. If you got it right, set that card aside.

In either case, *you will have gotten immediate feedback!*

F. Go on to the next card.

G. Your goal is to be able to look at the prefixes on all the cards, say the meanings *aloud*—and give sample words. This will help you not only pass the quizzes in this book but identify these prefixes wherever you see them.

15. Throughout the rest of this book, you will find the initials DRC in the right-hand margins. Word elements, affixes and roots will be listed under DRC.

<u>DRC</u>

ad-

Each time you see one of these, *immediately* stop and make a Data Retention Card for the word or word element listed.

NOTE: *Do not look at the back of a card before you have tried saying what's on the back.*

Then give yourself *immediate* feedback as to the correctness of your response by checking with the back of the card.

16. If you are having trouble with any of the prefixes, go back to see how they were linked with words you may already know. On each list below add two or three words using these prefixes.

Chapter 2, Para. 6	Chapter 2, Para. 13	Chapter 2, Para. 6
pre- (before)	**bi-** (two)	**a-, an-** (not, without)
pre-bedtime	bigamist	aversive
prehistoric	bicycle	anarchy
pregnant	bimonthly	atypical
prejudice	biannual	a-social
predisposition	bipartisan	amoral
preposition	biplane	atheist
_____	_____	_____
_____	_____	_____
_____	_____	_____

Chapter 2, Para 13

mono- (one)
monogamist
monarchy
monoplane
mononucleosis

_____

_____

_____

Chapter 2, Para. 18

trans- (across)
transient
transfer
transcribe
transmission

_____

_____

_____

Chapter 2, Para. 18

sub- (under)
subway
submarine
subpoena
subordinate

_____

_____

_____

Chapter 3, Para. 12

ad- (to, towards)
admission
advance
adhesive

_____

_____

_____

Chapter 2, Para. 18

auto- (self)
automobile
autonomy
autograph

_____

_____

_____

Chapter 2, Para. 6

non- (not)
non-aversive
nonsense
non-sequitur

_____

_____

_____

Chapter 4, Para. 12

ex- (out of)
ex-wife
ex-husband

_____

_____

_____

Chapter 2, Para. 13

poly- (many)
polygamy
polywogs

_____

_____

_____

Chapter 2, Para. 8

re- (back, again)
remission
recognize

_____

_____

_____

22. **NOTE:** The word *sophisticated* is an interesting one. It means "wise," from the root **sopho** and is used in such words as:

> sophomore (a wise fool)
> philosophy (love of wisdom)
> sophist (a skilled or clever person—
> who may be given to playing tricks)

Check your Data Retention Cards to see if your sample words are the best you can find for remembering the meanings of the prefixes.

17. It's rather like the multiplication tables in that some memorization is involved. Only these Data Retention Cards are easier; you can use words you already know to help you. You can *link the unknown to what you already know. You discover at once whether you are on the right track.*

DRC
un-

18. You may have been asking: How can I tell when word elements are affixes (either prefixes or suffixes) or roots? You know that one kind of affix, the prefix, comes *before* the root; the other kind, the suffix, comes *after* the root. But how can you tell if affixes are used at all? Well, after you have learned a dozen or so prefixes, you will find you are generally able to spot them—and other prefixes—as they occur.

19. Besides, being able to identify which are affixes and which are roots is not nearly as helpful as knowing the meaning of these common Greek and Latin word elements.

20. You will be amazed at how often they appear on the front page or the sports page of your newspaper, in business and technical conversations, and in textbooks.

21. Incidentally, the Data Retention Card system is an excellent device for retaining all kinds of data:

> Names of rocks for a geology course
> Musical terms—allegro, staccato, fortissimo
> Names and dates of rulers, historical events

Any data that requires simple identification and recall of information and that can be broken down into manageable (easily learned) elements can be put on Data Retention Cards for speedy learning.

22. Once you know the information, once you *have* the data, then you can go on to more sophisticated uses. Get some data, know that your body of data is right—and take off from there.

23. You have Data Retention Cards made up for all the prefixes-to-date, except those for which you are *absolutely* sure. Now is a good time to stop and make up DRCs for all roots that have been dealt

Answer Key

24.

duc, duct	to lead	
gamy	marriage	
gnos	knowledge	
logy	study of, science of	
miss, mitt	to send	
pli, plic	to fold	
pon, pos	to put or place	
port	to carry	
psych	mind	
scrib	to write	
spect	to look	
tain, ten	to hold	
vers, vert	to turn	

with so far in this text. Remember, the easiest way to show on your DRCs which are roots, which prefixes and which suffixes is by doing what? _____

_____

_____

(If you have forgotten, refer to paragraph 11 of this chapter, and then fill in blank above.)

24. Below is a list of some of the most frequently used roots that have appeared in this text so far. Next to the root is a sample word to aid you in writing in the root's meaning. If you do not know the meaning, you can refer to the chapter and paragraph number listed in the third column. Try to write in the meanings for all the roots.

Root	Sample Word	Chapter-Paragraph	Meaning of Root
Duc, duct	con**duct**or	2-8	_____
Gamy	mono**gamy**	2-13	_____
Gnos	reco**gni**tion	4-7	_____
Logy	bio**logy**	2-12	_____
Miss, mitt	com**miss**ion, com**mitt**ed	3-9	_____
Pli, plic	com**plic**ated	3-44	_____
Pon, pos	com**pon**ent, com**pos**ition	3-45	_____
Port	re**port**er	3-43	_____
Psych	**psych**osis	2-10	_____
Scrib	**scrib**ble	3-17	_____
Spect	**spect**ators	3-16	_____
Tain, ten	de**tain**, re**ten**tion	4-5	_____
Vers, vert	**vers**ion, **vert**ical	3-4	_____

Answer Key

26. 1. before
    2. after
    3. **cognos or gnos**
    4. knowledge
    5. away from knowledge; outside of knowledge
    6. away from God, outside of knowledge about God
    7. study of, or science of; study of God
    8. turn under, or to overthrow
    9. turning away, or turning against
    10. keep, or hold
    11. holding down
    12. move away from, apart from tension
    13. **ten:** hold
    14. "holds fast to things; has "stick-to-it-tive-ness"
    15. held (unbelievable)

Check your answers with the answer key at the bottom of page 76. Make up DRCs for any roots about which you are uncertain. Sometimes, just writing out the card fixes the root in your mind so that you will not forget it (using your kinetic sense!).

25. After you have made up your cards, go over them just as you were instructed to do with prefixes in paragraph 14 of this chapter.

26. Check over all your DRCs, prefixes *and* roots, and then try this quiz.

    1. **Pre**fixes come—or are fixed before ( ) or after ( ) the root?

    2. **Suffixes**, then, are where? Before ( ) or after ( ) the root?

    3. The word recognition has what root in it?_____.

    4. What does the root in number 3 mean?_____.

    5. An agnostic is one who is _____ .

    6. An atheist is one who is _____.
    (Remember that **theos** is a root meaning God.)

    7. **Logy** means _____ . Theology then means _____(or more generally, the study of religion).

    8. To subvert is to _____.

    9. An aversion to something is a _____.

    10. Data Retention Cards are small cards you make up to retain or _____ various kinds of data.

    11. Detention is the act of _____.

    12. Detente, on the other hand, means _____.

    13. Tenable, tenacious, tenant all have the same root: _____, meaning _____.

    14. A person who has tenacity would be one who (check one): ( ) gives up quickly, ( ) or holds fast to things, has "stick-to-it-tive-ness."

    15. A belief that is untenable is a belief that is *not* capable of being

_____.

DRC
Roots
duct
gamy
gnos
logy
miss
plic
pon
port
psych
scrib
spect
tain
vert

Answer Key

27. 1. Il Duce: one who *leads*
    2. Replica: "fold again" or an exact copy—usually made
        by the original artist
    3. Emit: "send out"
    4. Expound: "place outside of"
    5. Portable: carried

Check your answers with the answer key at bottom of the left-hand page (p. 78).

27. These are primarily word elements appearing, or reappearing, in this chapter. Now go over your DRCs again, and then try this second check-up quiz.

    1. The Second World War Italian leader, Mussolini, was called Il Duce, meaning one who _____ .

    2. A replica is a copy or reproduction of a work of art; replica means literally _____ .
                   (plic)   (re-)

    3. Emit uses two word elements, ex- plus **mitt**; it means literally

    _____ .
      (mitt)   (ex-)

    4. Expound links **ex-** with the root **pon**. It means "to explain in detail," or literally to _____ .
                 (pon)   (ex-)

    5. Do not mix the terms: potable water with portable water. Potable means "drinkable," while **port**able means "able to be

    _____ ." All water is portable in small enough quantities, but *not* all water is potable.

Check your answers with the answer key at the bottom of the left-hand page. Did you find this one more difficult than the earlier quiz? That may be because the literal meaning of a word is sometimes hard to figure out from what you know to be the accepted meaning. Replica, for example, in careful usage refers only to a copy done by the original artist. How do we get "fold again" from that? Perhaps because in botany, a replicate refers to a leaf that is folded back upon itself. But the word replica now can refer to any copy or reproduction.

28. As you have used roots in various ways so far in this text, you have no doubt noticed that the endings, or suffixes, change around. For example, notice the following various suffixes that all can be attached to the root **ten**:

Suffix	Makes
-able	tenable (adj.)
-acious	tenacious (adj.)
-ant	tenant (noun)
-sion	tension (noun)
-acity	tenacity (noun)

You will have more work on these suffixes in Chapter 5. But for now, remember the suffix comes *after* the root and changes it in some way, giving it a new direction.

29. You are very familiar with the suffix -s which forms the plural— more than one—of most nouns: boy, boys; table, tables; book, books; belief, beliefs. In fact, one of the best ways to spot nouns in our language is to see if we form the plural by adding -s or -es, as from the list of nouns above:

One	More than one
tenant	tenants
tension	tensions
tenacity	tenacities (y change to i and add **-es**.)

Why is it important to recognize nouns in vocabulary study? Well, you want to say:

That belief is tenable (capable of being held).

or

She has tenacity (stick-to-it-tive-ness).

not

That belief is tenacity (which would be incorrect). Most of the time you learn this merely from the place of the word in the sentence. But when you learn suffixes, it is wise to be sure you know—can **recognize**—which suffixes are used to form nouns and which to form other parts of speech in your sentences or phrases.

30. You have now dealt with prefixes, roots, and to a limited extent, suffixes. Note that the word suffix combines the prefix **sub-** with the root **fix**. Why don't we say and write **subfix** then? Or why don't we say and write adfix rather than affix, since **ad-** is the prefix, not really **af-**? (**Ad-**, as you know, means "to" or "toward.")

DRC
ad-

31. Because, in some respects, we are lazy language users. And we change our language all the time. If you have read Shakespeare, or a newspaper from 100 years ago—or if you have laughed about slang expressions that are from one to five years old—you are aware of the changes. Our language does not stand still; it moves with us.

32. So if we are somewhat lazy and if we can also make changes in the way we speak and write, we are not likely to keep on saying **subfix**. Try it aloud. Say subfix and then say suffix.

Notice the greater action required of the lips in the first way. Writing records speech! Therefore, in many cases, spelling of words mimics the speaking of these words.

33. We change the endings of some prefixes, but not of others. Study the following examples to see if you can figure out why some change and others do not.

Some prefixes that do *not* change:	Some prefixes that *do* change
Pre- as in predestiny	**Ad-** (meaning "to" or "toward") changes to **ac-** in accept
	to **af-** in affluent
Bi- as in biopsy	to **ag-** in aggrandize
Re- as in returnable	to **al-** in allotment
	to **an-** in annul
	to **ap-** in apposition
	to **ar-** in arrear
	to **as-** in associate
	to **at-** in attribute
	Ex- changes to **e-** in emission
	to **ec-** in eccentric
	to **ef-** in effete
	Sub- changes to **suf-** in suffix
	to **sup-** in suppression
	to **suc-** in succumb

Do you notice that the three prefixes above that do *not* change all end in vowels—in these cases either *e* or *i*. And that the three prefixes above that *do* change all end in consonants—*d, x,* or *b?* There is no purpose in changing the ones that end in vowels, because it is not difficult to pronounce the next part of the word. But when the prefix ends with *d, x, b, n, m,* or some other consonant, then that's different.

34. So **sub-** becomes **suf-**. The end of the prefix becomes the same as the beginning of the root—as in **suf**fix. This is *very* important in vocabulary building. You will find that your knowledge of prefixes will be much more valuable to you because you know about his change. For example: change the *d* in the prefix **ad-** to match the first letter in the root of the following words. (What does **ad-** mean? _____)

    1. **Ad-** plus sertion becomes _____ assertion _____

    2. **Ad-** plus sociation (social) becomes _____

    3. **Ad-** plus tribute (tribe: to bestow) becomes _____

    4. **Ad-** plus probation (prove) becomes _____

    5. **Ad-** plus similation (similar) becomes _____

    Check your responses with the list below.

35. Notice how the knowledge of prefixes helps with spelling. You have two consonants—two *s*'s, two *t*'s, two *p*'s—at the beginning in each case—since the prefix ends in a consonant and the root begins with a consonant (*s,t,* or *p*).

36. Notice that the word atone has only one consonant at the beginning. If the prefix comes from **ad-**, what do you suppose the root is?_____ The word means "to make up for something," "to make amends" or, literally, to make "at one."

37. Now try matching these five words using the prefix **ad-** with the appropriate meanings (**ad-** plus propriate becomes appropriate).

    1. An assertion   _____ a quality of characteristic said of someone

    2. An association   _____ a group of people

    3. An attribute   _____ approval

    4. An approbation   _____ a statement of supposed fact

    5. An assimilation   _____ making alike, absorbing

38. You can watch for many other words that use a changed form of the prefix **ad-** besides those of **as-**, **at-** and **ap-**. You will also find that **ad-** changes to:

Meaning

Ac-	accelerate	to speed up
Af-	affluent	wealth (flowing to you)
Ag-	aggravate	irritate (to "bug" someone)
Al-	allocate	to give out, to divide, to distribute
An-	annihilate	to destroy, to kill
Ar-	arrears	behind (in payments, usually)

39. Also note that **ad**here and **ad**hesive (meaning "to stick to") do *not* change. That is, we don't say or write "ahhere." Why not? Because sometimes the *h* is more like a vowel; it is a soft and easy-flowing sound.

40. Many words you are familiar with use this method of changing the prefix ending to agree with the beginning of the root. For example:

  Support links **sub-** and **port** (to carry)
  Suppose links **sub-** and **pose** (to put or place)

Can you record any others, using various forms of **ad-** and **sub-** and adding the rest to make words you already know:

Words using some form of **ad-**	Words using some form of **sub-**
(ac-, af-, ag-, al-, an-, ap-, ar-, as-, at-)	(suc-, sud-, suf-, sug-, sum-, sup-)

41. **In-, in-**

Two other prefixes—spelled just the same but meaning almost the opposite—also take on several prefix changes. These are:

  In- meaning *not,* and
  In- meaning *highly* or *within*

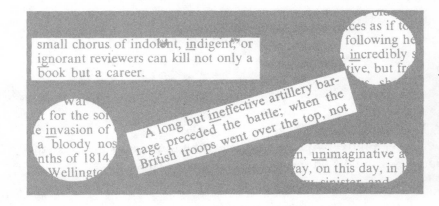

Answer Key
44. In- plus literate = Illiterate
In- plus luminate = Illuminate

Remember seeing the word **inflammable** on some aerosol or gasoline cans? It has recently been replaced by "highly flammable" because too often people thought inflammable meant *not* flammable or not capable of flame. Flammable means *very* or *highly* flammable. Confusing the meaning of the prefixes can lead to disaster!

42. How can you tell which prefix is being used? Does innate mean *not* natural or *highly* natural? Well, it means *highly* natural. Does inborn mean *not* born? No, it means *born into*—"ingrained." *Not* born is unborn. Now you know that **un-** means "not." So we have: **un**natural (not natural), **un**conscious (not conscious), **un**exposed (not exposed), **un**connected—and so on.

43. How can you tell? Sometimes only by checking your dictionary.

44. **In-** and **in-** change their spellings, too.

Illegal, as you know, means *not* legal. So **in-** can change to **il-** before words beginning with *l*. Not literate then would be written

_____ . To write one word meaning that something was *highly* luminated (provided with light), on the other hand,

would be to say that it was _____ .

Here are a few examples of **in-** used both ways:

In- meaning *not*	**In-** meaning *highly* or *within*
Inanimate: not animated or lively—no cartoons	Inaugurate: a formal introduction into something
Inadvisable: not advisable, don't do it	Incarcerate: to shut in
Inarticulate: not clear, not articulated so it communicates	Induction: to be led into
Inaudible: not audible, not capable of being heard	
Infinite: not finite, having no boundaries or limits	

Which do the following mean—*not* or *highly?*

If you are not sure, look them up *immediately.*

Answer Key

44. Invisible: *not* visible
Insignificant: *not* significant
Involuntary: *not* voluntary
Innate: born *into*, natural
Inborn: born *into*, inescapable

45. **Ad-** as in advance, adhesive
In- as in innate, inborn
In- as in incredible, invisible
Un- as in unchangeable, unasked . . . *and many more.*
Check your dictionary
Ten, tain, as in untenable, retainable
Gnos, as in recognition, agnostic
Check your dictionary if you are in doubt about words
that may come from these roots.

N—88

Invisible

Insignificant

Involuntary

Innate

Inborn

45. You have now added the prefixes (fill in blanks)

ad- meaning "to" or "toward" as in _____

in- meaning "into" or "highly" as in _____

in- meaning "not" as in _____

un- meaning "not" as in _____

to your growing list of prefixes, and the roots

ten, tain meaning "to hold" as in _____

gnos meaning "knowledge" as in _____

to your growing list of roots.

(A) You have learned how to make and use Data Retention Cards. Keep them with you, studying them at stop lights, bus stops, or while waiting for the phone to ring. Checking up on yourself, getting immediate feedback on how you are doing, is vital to your vocabulary growth.

(B) You have learned about the spelling changes in many prefixes (those ending with consonants). This will greatly aid your ability to identify and use the prefixes you know, giving you immediate ability to recognize many words you might otherwise miss.

46. NOTE: Chances are that you have not yet made up Data Retention Cards for the following word elements:

DRC
bio
de-

bio meaning "life"
de- meaning "down" or "away"

Have you seen the term **bio-degradable**? It appears on some washing powder boxes and simply means that the substances in the box can be returned to nature, that the pollution factor is low.

Make up Data Retention Cards for these two, using **biode**gradable, **bio**logy, **de**press, **de**tach—or any other words of your choosing as sample words.

47. NOTE: Before going to the next chapter, *Practice Frequently*, which is closely linked to this chapter, take the following check-up quiz. Go over your DRCs first so you will be sure to succeed!

Chapter 4: Check-up Quiz

Instructions: Write down the prefix and the root in each of the following words, and give the meaning for each.

Word	Prefix	Meaning
Detain		
Recognize		
A-logical		
Non-versatile		
Prepossess		
Explicate		
Prescribe		
Submissive		
Transported		
Monogamy		
Transducer		
Inspection		
Invertible		

Word	Root	Meaning
Detain		
Recognize		
A-logical		
Non-versatile		
Prepossess		
Explicate		
Prescribe		
Submissive		
Transported		
Monogamy		

Word	Root	Meaning
Biopsychology		
Transducer		
Inspection		
Invertible		
Tenable		

Check your responses with the table below. If you missed any, go through your Data Retention Cards and pull out the cards for the prefixes or roots you missed. Study these carefully before you attempt the check-up quiz that is on the tear-out sheet at the back of the book. If you missed none of the above—or only one or two—try the check-up quiz on this chapter at the back of the book.

Word	Prefix	Meaning
Detain	De-	down, away
Recognize	Re-	back, again
A-logical	A-	outside of
Non-versatile	Non-	not
Prepossess	Pre-	before
Explicate	Ex-	out of, formerly
Prescribe	Pre-	before
Submissive	Sub-	under
Transported	Trans-	across
Monogamy	Mono-	one
Transducer	Trans-	across
Inspection	In-	in, into
Invertible	In-	not

Word	Root	Meaning
Detain	Tain, ten	to hold
Recognize	Gognos, gnos	to know
A-logical	Logos	to study, the science of

Words	Root	Meaning
Non-versatile	**Vers, vert**	to turn
Prepossess	**Pos, pon**	to put or place
Explicate	**Plic**	to fold
Prescribe	**Scrib**	to write
Submissive	**Miss, mitt**	to send
Transported	**Port**	to carry
Monogamy	**Gamy**	marriage
Biopsychology	**Bio**	life
	Psych	mind, behavior
	Logy	to study, the science of
Transducer	**Duc**	to lead
Inspection	**Spect**	to look
Invertible	**Vert, vers**	to turn
Tenable	**Ten**	to hold

If you are having trouble remembering any of the word elements, check your dictionary *and* the page in this text where the word was first used. The index at the back of this text will refer you to the proper page.

Practice Frequently

1. When you meet people whom you don't want to forget, you probably:

   (A) Make sure you heard their names correctly in the first place.

   (B) Repeat their names to yourself so you'll remember them. In other words, you practice. If you get a phone number you don't want to forget, you probably say the number over to yourself—aloud—while you are looking for a piece of paper on which to write the number. You practice the number.

2. And so with words. If you *want* to remember new words, you need to practice them. You need to look at them, say them aloud, analyze them, and think about their meanings. That's why you have Data Retention Cards.

3. Learning experts tell us that we learn most things best if we have frequent, short learning sessions rather than infrequent, long ones. If you don't think about those attractive people you meet for a week or so, you may have forgotten their names. If you think about them—or him or her—the next day, or an hour after learning their names, chances are you'll remember.

4. In the last chapter you encountered the word **theos**. Do you remember what it means? _____ And **logy**, do you remember what it means? _____
   If you have a brother-in-law who is a theologian, or if you are thinking about taking a course in biology, possibly you did remember them. Or if you said them aloud, thought about them, practiced them, chances are you remembered them. A theologian is one who studies about God, or about religion in general; biology is the study of life; **bio-**, as you recall, means "life."

5. **NOTE:** Don't confuse edifice with oedipus:

edifice—pronounced ed-uh-**fuss**, meaning "a building"

oedipus—pronounced both ed-uh-**pus** and ede-uh-**pus**, referring to a figure from ancient Greece who killed his father and married his mother.

5. You may have linked the unknown to the known in these instances. You got immediate feedback from the page about the meaning of the words. Your next step, then, is to practice frequently. So, let's detail it.

(A) You know how to make up DRCs. Carry them with you—in your shirt pocket, in your purse, or if you are in school, inside the cover of a book you carry.

If you haven't already made up DRCs on **theos** and **logy**, do so now. Some good sample words would be:

theos (God)	Theology	**DRC**
	Atheist	**theos**
logy (study of or science of)	Biology	**DRC**
	Criminology	**logy**

(B) Look at them at *any* free moment—tooth brushing time, waiting for the bus time; put them on the visor of your car and check one at a time while the stop light is red. Look at them while you are waiting for class to begin or for your coffee to cool.

(C) Add new cards—from this text, from your job, from the newspaper, television, from any source at all. For example, this morning's sports page had the word edifice (about the New Orleans Sports Complex); a recent issue of *Life* has the phrase monetary gyrations. In an *Ebony* article appears the word enigmatic. If you are interested, look them up, put them on DRCs, link them to words you already know.

(D) Look at the DRCs every day. Or better, twice a day. Put aside the cards you know and check them at the end of the week.

(E) At any possible time, try to recall the prefixes, roots, new words you studied from the chapter you just read. Then try to link them with other words you know.

6. Try these:

1. **Logy** means _____

   Socio means "society" (social, socialism).

   So Sociology means _____

   How about asocial? _____ antisocial: _____

6. **NOTE:** Why couldn't someone who writes about various beliefs in God be called a **theographer?** It's possible—only we have called those who write about the nature of God "apostles," "prophets," "theologians." We just haven't had a need for the word theographer—yet.

N—98

2. **Astro** means "star"; astrology has to do with the _____ of the stars, only that term is not as "studious" or scientific as the word astronomy, which refers to the careful study of the universe beyond the earth.

   DRC
   astro

   It is curious that we translate the Russian term for men who travel in space as cosmonauts, **cosmos** meaning "world." And

   our men who travel into space we call _____.

   DRC
   cosmos

3. **Graph**, you'll recognize, as a word meaning "writing."
   Graphite is the name for pencil lead.

   DRC
   graph

   Graphology means _____ (now generally called graphoanalysis or the study of handwriting to diagnose personal characteristics).

   And autograph means _____.

   Biography means _____.

   How about autobiography? _____

   Check your answers with answer key at bottom of left-hand page.

Now practice:

Bio	means	_____
Theos	means	_____
Graph	means	_____
Logy	means	_____
Astro	means	_____
Socio	means	_____

DRC
socio

Check your answers with answer key. Miss any? Make up a DRC for any one of the roots you missed, if you haven't done so already. Put the meaning of the root and an example of the word using the root on the back of each card.

7. Studying some contrasting prefixes, linking them with roots, and practicing them frequently will help you fix them in your memory. For example: **intra-, inter-,** and **inner.**

Answer Key

7. (a) **intra-** means "within"

(b) **inter-** means "between," "among"

(c) between races

(d) between religions

(e) within the uterus

(f) within the psyche (or mind)

(g) **vert** means "to turn"

(h) **introvert**: turned within

(i) **extrovert**: turned outside of

(j) **introspection**: to look within

(k) **intra-, intro-, inner-**: within

(l) **intra-, intro-, inner**: inside of

(m) **inter-**: between

at the Massachu
to develop a s
he interrelated t
atural nonrenew
iculture includi

Intra-mural sports are "within the walls" (within the college, for example). **Mural** means "wall." We use the word **mural** to refer to wall hangings, especially those showing a scene or landscape. **Inter-** means "between," so **intermural** sports are those that occur *between* walls, or between colleges or high schools. So **intra-** means (a)

_____ ; and **inter-** means (b) _____ . Interracial means (c)_____ ; **interreligious** means

(d) _____ . An **intrauterine** device (IUD) is one that is placed (e)_____ the female's uterus in order to prevent pregnancy. **Intrapsychic** means (f) _____ .
Intra- means the same as **intro-**, as in **introvert**.

Remember, **vert** is a root meaning (g) _____ ? So **introvert** means (h) _____ . Which leads us to its opposite: **extrovert**. **Ex-**, you know, means "out of." **Extro-** is the same; an **extrovert** is one who (i)_____. Which do you prefer being around, introverts or extroverts? Or some of each? Then there is **introspection**. What does that mean? You know the word **spectacles** (looking glasses), **spectator**, and **inspection**? Remember, **spect** means "to look" (inspection: to look into something). Therefore, **introspection** is (j) _____

_____ —specifically, to look within one's self.

Are mature people introspective, capable of looking inside themselves? Of taking responsibility for their own behavior? Then there is **inner-** or "inside of," as in **inner**-city, **inner**-feelings. So **intra-**, **intro-**, **inner-** all mean (k) _____ or (l) _____

_____ , and **inter-** means (m) _____ .
Check answers with answer key at bottom of left-hand page.

8. **Hypo-** and **hyper-**: A **hypodermic** needle is one that goes *inside* the *skin.* (**Derm** is the Greek word for skin.) **Hypo-** means "under" or "below." **Hyper-** is the opposite, so it means (a) _____

_____ . **Hypo**-active means (b) _____ and **hyperactive** means (c) _____ . A person who has a **hypothy-**

9. **NOTE:** Another word that is hard to figure out, as far as spelling goes, is promiscuous, which generally refers to someone who is not very choosy about a sexual partner. It *sounds* almost as if the word began with the prefix **per-**. One thing that helps is to try changing the ending of the word—promiscuous to promiscuity (or the adjective to the noun). Often this tells you where to search for a word in the dictionary.

roid condition has an (d) _____ -active thyroid; conversely, the person who has a **hyper**thoid condition has an (e) _____ -active thyroid. Someone who is **hyper**sensitive would be (f) _____ sensitive. A statement that is placed *under* other statements—or theses—would be called an (g) _____ thesis. That is, it is a kind of statement underneath others, upon which others are built.

9. **Pre-, per-, pro-:** Pre- means (a) _____ . Per- means "thoroughly," "through" and "away"—among other things. It has too many meanings to make it very beneficial, but then you can always check specific words with your dictionary: **Pro-** can mean "before," just like **pre-**; it can also mean "favoring" or "supporting." So we have:

DRC
per-
pro-

> **Prophylactic**—meaning "to keep guard beforehand," to guard ahead of time against disease.
>
> **Procreate**—"to support creation," especially by producing off-spring, having kids, begetting progenitors.

Don't confuse the prefix **pro-** with the abbreviation for professional, as in **pro**-football.

Be canny also about the *pro*'s and *con*'s of things. The **pro** *does* mean "in favor of or supporting," but the **con** does *not* come from the prefix meaning "with." The *pro*'s and *con*'s are the fors and againsts. Can you think of any words using the prefix **per-**? Write in as many as you can on the following left-hand page; then check with the list below.

Here are a few common words using **per-**:

perfect	perforate	perspective
pertinent	performance	persuade
personna gratis	percolate	persecute
permanent	percent	permit

You may wish to check your dictionary for any you have listed that are not listed here. There are *many* more. But sometimes it is difficult to tell by listening to the word whether or not the spelling is **per-**, **pro-**, or **pre-**. How about the fancy, four-syllable word meaning "to lie," for example. How is it spelled? _____ varicate. Well, it's **pre-**. (To vary **before**hand?)

Following is a brief review of prefixes: Paragraph

    Inter- means   _____   7

    Intra- means   _____   7

    Hypo- means   _____   8

    Hyper- means   _____   8

    Pre- means   _____   9

    Pro- means   _____   9

As an abbreviation:

    Pro- stands for _____   9

Check your answers with answer key. If you missed any, return to that particular paragraph and reread the meanings of the prefixes. Now try this short check-up quiz. Fill in the blanks with the term that corresponds to the meaning below the line:

1. The _____ mediate groups are playing _____ mural sports.
        (between)   (within)

2. Just the sight of a _____ dermic needle makes me _____ sensi-
                  (under)   (very)
tive.

3. Two prefixes that mean "before" are _____ and _____ ; one
                                   (before)   (before)

    also means favoring _____ .
                   (favoring)

4. Both the Russian _____ nauts and the American _____ nauts
                  (world)   (star)
    have flown into space.

Check your answers with the answer key.

Go over your Data Retention Cards carefully to be sure you have cards for terms filled into blanks above. Be sure your sample words on the backs of the cards are good ones—that is, helpful to *you*.

And practice them frequently.

10. **Com-, con-, col-, cor-: Com-** means "with." So does **con-** (as a prefix) and so do **col-** and **cor-**. They all mean "with" or "to-

10. **NOTE:** Again you can reap unexpected spelling helps from knowing prefixes. As commiserate has two *m*'s, so does:

> correlate have two *r*'s (**com-** plus relate)
> colleague have two *l*'s (**com-** plus league)
> corrode have two *r*'s (**com-** plus rode).

"You and your colleagues (fellow workers) can correlate (bring together) your ideas on the corrosion (wearing away) of the commune (living together)."

Commune is an easy word. It comes from the word common, which links **com-** with a very old word meaning "public." Now we have: common law, common denominator, common sense, communication, communion, communist, community, communize—and many more!

gether," a happy prefix. Well, sometimes happy. You know the word "misery"? Add the prefix **com-** and you get commiserate: to feel miserable together. Perhaps it is best to be miserable *with* someone rather than alone. Less miserable that way? Okay, so in that sense **com-** still is a "happy" prefix.

DRC
com-

"Togetherness" may or may not be a happy idea (com-ness?). But **communication** is—when what one communicates really gets across. And so can a combo be a happy idea (short for **combination**). So

com- is a prefix meaning _____ .

As the prefix **ad-** changes to agree with the root, so does the prefix **com-** change to agree with the roots following it. You know what a lateral pass is? A pass "to the side"? Well, **collateral** is something that is "on the side *with* something"—as a collateral loan (you put something *with* something. You say, "If I don't pay, I will give up this thing which I put on the side.").

Again, your spelling is aided by your knowledge of prefixes: You write two *l*'s in collateral because you have the prefix **com-** (changed to **col-**) and the root **lateral.** You have two *m*'s in commiserate because the prefix **com-** is linked to the root **miserate.**

Now link **com-** to relate and you get _____ .

Colleague links _____ and _____ .

Corrode (rodent, "to gnaw") links_____ and _____ .

11. **Homo-, hetero-: Homo sapiens** means "thinking man." **Sapiens** being a word for "thinking" and **homo** for "man." But **homo-** has another meaning. Homogenized milk, for example, can be consumed by cats as well as by men—it simply means "all the same," that is, the same fat content throughout. The prefix **homo-**, therefore, means "same." **Hetero-** is the *opposite* of **homo-; hetero-**

DRC
homo-
hetero-

means _____ . **Hetero-**sexual activities are activities with persons of

_____the same sex

_____different sex

In this chapter alone, you have been introduced to eleven prefixes which are listed on page 109. Some are antonyms (opposites): **inter/intra; hyper/hypo; homo/hetero. Pre-, pro-, per-** are variants of the

Answer Key

12. **hyper-:** over, very
hypo-: under
inter-: between
intra-: within
homo-: same
hetero-: different
pre-: before
pro-: through, away, thoroughly
com-: with
   (col-, con-, cor-)

13. 1. hyperactive
   hypo-active
   interactive
   2. produce, production
   conduct, conductor
   (note: introduce comes from **in-** plus **duc**)
   3. comportment—same as deportment,
   (old terms for "conduct")
   4. colleague (college, collegiate),
   interleague, intra-league

same form. And **com-** merely has several spellings—**col-, con-,** or **cor-** depending on root following the prefix.

Inter-	Hyper-	Pre-	Com-	Homo-
Inner-	Hypo-	Pro-	(col-)	Hetero-
Intra-		Per-	(con-)	
			(cor-)	

12. Practicing these frequently will imprint them in your mind so that whenever you see them, you will know them. Give yourself a fast review by filling in the meanings for each of these words.

Prefix	Meaning	Prefix	Meaning
Hyper-		Pre-	
Hypo-		Pro-	
Inter-		Per-	
Intra-		Com-	
Homo-		Col-	
Hetero-		Cor-	

13. Now link as many of the prefixes as you can—still making sense—to the following roots:

1. Which ones can you link to **active: hyperactive** _____

_____

2. Which ones can you link to **duct** or **duction** (lead): _____

_____

3. Which ones can be linked to **port** (carry): _____

_____

4. Which ones can be linked to **league** (association): _____

_____

Check your answers with the answer key. If you missed any, make up Data Retention Cards—if you have not already done so. If you already have the cards, *practice them frequently.*

15. **NOTE:** A word that characterizes some conversations, Talk Shows, advertisements, and so forth is hyperbole (pronounced hi-purr-bow-lee). It refers to super-statements, exaggerations. "The most fantastic . . . the wildest . . . the grossest. . . ."

14. **Mnemonic devices:** One very good way to remember things is to make up your own mnemonic device. Don't let the word scare you. Examine it in context and try breaking it apart into manageable parts.

   (A) You know that you *don't* sound the *p* in pneumonia or in pneumatic; likewise, you don't sound the *m* in mnemonic—it's ne-mon-ic. Three syllables.

   (B) There is a hint of the word "memory" in mnemonic—**mnem**onic devices are "memory tricks."

   It is a good word to experiment with and try out on your friends. More importantly, using mnemonic devices can help you remember word meanings. For example, let's say you are having trouble remembering the difference between **hyper-** and **hypo-**. Well, what's a word that uses one of these two prefixes: **hypodermic needle?**

   Sure, "under" the skin. **Derm** is the medical term for "skin." So remembering that **hypodermic** means "under" the skin makes it possible for you to remember that **hypo-** means "under" and **hyper-** means "over."

15. Or it may be very easy for you to remember that a **hyper**active child is "very" active. Or **hyper**tension—or whatever you choose as your word for a memory trick.

16. This is just another way of saying "link the unknown to what you already know." But often it helps if you "play games" with the things you are trying to learn and sometimes come up with some weird combinations. More on this in Chapter 9.

17. Do you have trouble remembering that **com-**, **col-**, **con-**, and **cor-** are different forms of the prefix meaning "with?" What's your best mnemonic device for remembering this:

   colleague—one who works *with* you
   communicate—speaking *together*
   communist—bound *with* one another
   commiserate—being miserable *together*
   combat—to fight *with*
   conjoin—to join *with*

   Do you know magna *cum* laude—the Latin phrase for **commenda**tion? *With* (cum) *highest* (magna) *praise* (laude).

18. **NOTE: Fer** and **port** (both mean "to carry") can be linked to a variety of prefixes:

Fer	Port
auto-ferry	auto-port
deference	deportation
conference	comportment
infer	important
non-ferrous	non-portable
("ferrous" means "iron" in this case)	
offer	opportunity
preference	purport
	(The prefix **pur-** is like **pro-**.)
refer	report
suffer	support

Some of them have been used so much that their meanings have shifted; it's hard to figure out how **sub-** plus **fer** (suffer) meant "carry under," or how **ob-** plus **port** became opportunity. Besides **port** meaning "to carry," it also meant "harbor," or "portal." So opportunity came from the words meaning "to—or through—the harbor."

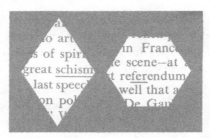

18. Mnemonic devices work for a great deal of the word elements: They need not be especially "far out."

    (A) **Gamy** means "marriage"—if you are "game" for it.

    (B) **Il Duce**, in Italian, means "the leader" as you read in Chapter 1. Mussolini was the Fascist leader during the Second World War—he was called "Il Duce."

    (C) The root **fer** is in ferry boat, which "carries one across" so **fer** means "to bear" or "carry."

        DRC
        fer

    (D) **Port**, also, means "to carry." Port wine can carry one into another state; can "transport" one, so to speak.

    Make up your own mnemonic devices; fit them to your style. But as you practice, link the things you have trouble remembering with things you already know.

19. Another good use for mnemonic devices—besides remembering meanings of word elements—is for remembering pronunciations.

20. Not much has been written thus far in this text about pronunciation. Primarily this is because the pronunciation of the Latin and Greek word elements is usually not very difficult. You may have some trouble with accent from time to time. But the safest way is simply to accent all syllables about the same. Let's call it the "Continental Technique." (Try *not* accenting any syllable in that last phrase: Con-ti-nen-tal Tech-nique.)

21. Generally, the Latin-Greek word elements don't give Americanized-English speakers much trouble. Some words do throw us. For example:

Chasm   Schism

In neither word do you pronounce the "h" so it's: chasm: (cah-zim) meaning a cave, an opening, a split, a rift. Your mnemonic device can be *cave.*

Schism: (siz-em) meaning a split, also; a separation—a cutting apart. Your mnemonic device can be *scis*sors.

So you have: chasm—a *cave* (cah-zim) and schism—cut by *scis*sors (siz-em). "You have created a **chasm** or **schism** by your dividing us; the resulting **schism** will forever leave a **chasm** in my heart." (Read it *aloud.*)

In this chapter you have added ten new prefixes, and learned or added to several roots. You have also been encouraged to *practice these* and your other word elements *frequently,* because short, frequent learning sessions will profit you most of all.

You have also learned, or re-learned, to link the things you want to learn with material that is already familiar to you by using mnemonic devices. These little memory tricks can be utilized in all sorts of ways outside of vocabulary building: remembering people's names, street names, foreign words and so on. But the key to it all is:

practice a little
then practice a little more,
then a

l
 i
  t
   t
    l
     e

      m
       o
        r
         e
          .
           .
            .

When you are ready, try the chapter quiz.

Chapter 5: Check-up Quiz

1. Practice the following roots by linking them with **logos** (or **logy**), meaning "to study" or "the science of." (**Logos** also means speech, reason.)

   Then give the meaning of the word you have formed.

Root	Plus **logos** (**logy**) makes	Meaning
Anthropo	Anthropology	the study of man
Theos		
Astro		
Cosmo		
Graph		
Socio		
Bio		
Derm (**Dermato**)		

2. What is a mnemonic device?

   Do you pronounce the first *m*?

3. Practice the following prefixes by making as many words as you can using them:

Inter-	Intra-	Hypo-	Hyper-

Pre-   Per-   Pro-   Com-
                                                    (Col-, con-, cor-)

Homo-   Hetero-   Extra-, extro-

Check your responses with the response sheet that follows.

Chapter 5: Check-up Quiz Completed

1. **Theology**: study of god or gods
    Astrology: study of heavenly bodies (stars)
    Cosmology: study of origin of the universe
    Graphology: study of hand-writing (now usually called graphoana-lysis)
    Sociology: study of societies, people in groups
    Biology: study of life, of living things
    Anthropology: study of man
    Dermatology: study of skin—and its disorders

2. A mnemonic device is a "memory trick" or an aid to remembering things. No, the first *m* is *not* pronounced.

3. Check your dictionary for any entries you made that are not listed below:

Inter-	Intra- (intro-)	Hypo-	Hyper-
interracial	intramural	hypodermic	hyperactive
interreligious	intrapsychic	hypoactive	hyperthyroid
inter-planetary	introspection	hypothesis	hypersensitive
	introvert	hypochondriac	hypertension

Pre-	Per-	Pro-	Com-
preserves	pertinent	prognosticate	commiserate
prepare	pervert	procreate	combo
preform	perforate	propaganda	correlate
prerequisite	percolate		colleague
preamble	permutation		corrode

Homo-	Hetero-	Extro- (extra-)
homogenized	hetergeneous	extrovert
homogeneous	heterosexual	extradition
homosexual	heterodox	extraordinary

When you are ready, take the tear-out quiz at the back of the book. But *practice* first!

Answer Key

5. 1. with
   2. self, self
   3. out of, out of
   4. back, again, back
   5. very
6. Prefix: **il- (in-)**, Root: **logy**, Suffix: **-al**; Bonus question: speaking well of someone

Chapter **6**

Reward Yourself

1. Most of us like doing those things that we do fairly well. You and I probably both prefer to practice things we are good at doing.

2. On the other hand, if you have had trouble with math, you probably don't "like" math or if you've never enjoyed English grammar, chances are you dislike English. Probably, the problem lies in what teachers and students all too often consider "English" to be.

3. We know from studying human behavior that we can be motivated to do things or that we can learn things in various ways, whether we like the things or not. We can be motivated by fear, threat, or punishment (aversive, negative stimuli). Or we can be motivated by joy, fun, reward (pleasant, positive stimuli). Most of us like to be rewarded—with praise or a good grade, with a raise in pay or a return favor. Obviously, these rewards come from others.

4. But how about rewarding *yourself*?

5. What would you like to do right now? Drink a coke? Call a friend? Take a nap? Read a book?

Try the quiz below and *reward yourself* if you do well. Right after you check your quiz, do something *you* want to do.

1. To **commiserate** is to feel miserable _____ someone.

2. **Auto-** means _____ , so an automobile is _____ -mobilized.

3. **Ex-** means _____ so an ex-officio member is one who is _____ office.

4. **Re-** means _____ so Data Retention Cards help you remember or bring data _____ .

119

5.   Someone who is **hyper**active is _____ active.

6.   The word **illogical** has a prefix, a root, and a suffix. What are they:

Prefix: _____ Root: _____ Suffix: _____

Does illogical mean *not* logical?

Now try this bonus question:

Eu- is a prefix meaning "good." You may remember that **logy** means "study of" or "science of." But is also means "writing or speaking about." So a eulogy is _____ .
When do eulogies usually occur? At funerals? Correct. Rarely do we hear unpleasant things about a person at his own funeral service!

Now check your answers with the answer key. How did you do? At least five out of six right? Great! Take a break.

6. The point is that *if* you will:

1.   be sure you've got your data straight *(get immediate feedback),*

2.   go over it in short intervals *(practice frequently);* you should then set up some rewards for yourself when you have accomplished what you set out to do.

7. If you missed any of the above, write the meaning of the prefix you missed—along with its meaning and a sample word—in the space below. Refer to the chapter and paragraph listed if you need to. *Then* take a shorter break.

Prefix	Meaning	Sample Word	Chapter-Paragraph
Auto-	_____	_____	2, 18
Ex-	_____	_____	4, 12
Re-	_____	_____	2, 8
Hyper-	_____	_____	5, 8
Eu-	_____	_____	6, 5
Com-	_____	_____	5, 10

DRC
eu-

8. Now, you may be one of these people who is rewarded most by learning more. Fine! In that case, go on. But don't forget:

>   Rewarding yourself can speed up your rate of learning and aid your retention of knowledge.

   Figure out your own rewards! What keeps your motor humming happily? And *use* these rewards when you think you have deserved them—often!

9. One reward from learning common prefixes, roots and suffixes comes with your new ability to recognize new words and word elements.

10. When you first saw the word wheels in Chapter 3, you may not have been able to recognize all of the prefixes. Take a look on pages 45-47. Now examine the prefixes in greater detail.

11. The prefixes **con-**, **sub-**, **per-** and **ad-** appear on both wheels:

Root: **Vert**	Root: **Miss**
Con-: to convert someone is to *turn* him so he agrees *with* you—conversion, a convert.	Commission means a variety of things—a fee for services, a task assigned. Check the **con**text.
Sub-: to subvert someone is to *under*mine his beliefs.	Sub mission means placing yourself *under* someone or something.
Ad-: to advertise is, hopefully, to *turn* someone's attention *to* you or your product.	Admission again depends on the context: a fee paid, to give into—complicated, you'll have to admit that!
Per-: to pervert someone is to turn him throughout, *thoroughly change* him.	Permission is **consent**, someone in authority granting you leave to do something.

12. Note the differences in the words **throughout** and **thoroughly** used in explaining pervert. The word, **through**, has how many syllables?_____ Did you write one? Right! Some day, say in another 100 years, it may be spelled "thru" in other than informal letter writing. The other one, thoroughly, has three syllables: thor-ough-ly (thir-o-ly) and means "completely, entirely, with great care." Five or six hundred years ago, they were the same word.

13. **Di-, in-, trans-, o-,** and **re-** are each used only on one of the wheels. Could these prefixes be *linked with* both words? Let's see:

Di-: To **divert** someone's attention is to "turn it away." The *s* has been dropped from the prefix **dis-,** which you can recognize in **disconnect, disjoin,** and so on. Can this be linked to the root **mis-**

sion on wheel 2? Sure—**dismiss, dismissal**—meaning _____ . School **dismissal** probably never seemed filled with **dismay.**

In-: Does **invert** mean "to turn into" or "not to turn?"

_____ . How do you know? Perhaps because you linked "in" with **introvert,** a person who is turned *inside* himself. Do we have **inmission** or **immission?** No, but we do have the similar-sounding word **emission** (**emit, eject**—"to throw out," since **ex-,** as you remember, means "out of." Here the *x* part is dropped, so the prefix is **e-,** "out of").

Trans-: You know **transmission,** "sending across"—as from the engine to a driving axle on a car. (**Transmitter, transmittal, transmit.**) **Transverse** means "crosswise." We have **transvestite,** too, but the root is **vest** (clothing). A transvestite is one who crosses over to the other sex in choice of clothes, a male dressing in female clothes and vice versa.

O-: is a form of **ob-** meaning "away, out." It frequently means other things—toward, before—so check your dictionary!

O-: We have **omission** and **omit** (to leave something *out*). We have **overt** (open and observable) behavior.

Re-: There is **revert** which means: _____ .

Also, **remit** which means: _____ .

(**Reverting, reversion, remittance, remission . . .**) turning back, or sending back.

We have noted earlier that the root **vert** "to turn" changes to the noun **verse** (a turning of prose), and that the root **mitt** "to send" changes to the noun **mission** (a sending).

14. Now, have you reread the above carefully? Then reward yourself. Have some fun by experimenting with the words and building your own set of wheels. You should do better—have more words on the spokes of your wheels—than the wheels on pages 58 and 59. All of the prefixes but one can be used to link with both roots.

DRC
o-
ob-

Circle the prefix that can only be linked to one root:

con-   ad-   dis- (di-)   trans-   re-

sub-   per-   in-   o-

Now, using that list of prefixes, and any others you care to, fill in the following word wheels:

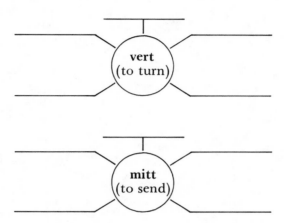

One of the ways to while away the time is to make up some word wheels of your own; how about the root **ten**, "to hold," or its other form **tain**. What prefixes can you add to it?

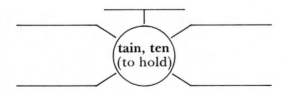

Remember that prefix endings change, **sub-** can become **sus-**, for example. Do you know the word sustenance? (food—enough to main**tain** life) Now how about maintenance—main**tain** and mainten-ance—both forms for the root **ten—tain**.

Did you get lost on that last one? This kind of experimenting with words *can* be rewarding.

15. Reread the last paragraph; you have:

   maintenance   and   maintain
      (noun)   (verb)

   sustenance—and you know sustain?

How about: retention and _____

Can you think of others:

Any using the prefix **de-**?

_____ and _____

Now check your word wheels with the material below, and your answers to the blanks above with the answer key on page 124.

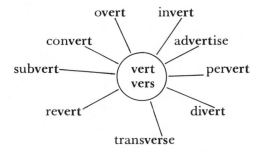

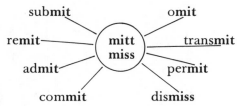

(only one *t* when used as verb)

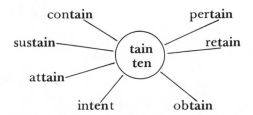

11. **NOTE:** It is curious that convert and conversion have to do with changing someone so that he agrees *with* you, but that conversely means "the opposite of," or "on the other side." Of course, all of these, plus convertible and converter, suggest turning something *around.* Convergence, on the other hand, has to do with a union, or a coming together.

16. com-, con-
col-
sub-

ad-
per-
de-
in-
in-
trans-
di-, dis-
re-

communicate, colleague
suboceanic, subterranean
subjugate

adhere, alledged
pervasive, pervert
detain, defer
infer, invert
insane, inferior
transfer, transmit
digest, dismiss
refer, remiss, retain

16. Back to the wheel. You now have learned many prefixes and many roots. Let's *recapitulate* (capture again? not quite that, literally, but the general meaning is *restate.*) Recapitulate has five syllables: re-ca-pi-tu-late. So to recapitulate or restate the prefixes used on the word wheels in Chapter 3 and again in this chapter, fill in the blanks below. You will notice that this time the *meanings* have been given, not the prefix itself:

Prefix	Meaning	Sample Word
	with, together with	
	under	
	to, toward	
	thoroughly	
	down, away from	
	in, into or not	
	across	
	away, out	
	back, again	

Check your answers with answer key. You may want to check your dictionary if you have sample words that are not listed in the answer key.

17. If you miss some or any of these, turn to your Data Retention Cards and pull out the prefixes that you missed. Spend a few minutes reviewing them. Look at card, *say aloud* what is on the back (meaning, sample word). Then cover up the prefixes above with a piece of scratch paper and write on that piece of paper the prefixes that you missed.

18. Now sit back and take a look at how you are doing. Ask yourself these questions:

   1. Do I practice my Data Retention Cards often? Do I especially go over the ones with which I am having trouble?

   Yes _____ No _____

2. Do I look for—and find—prefixes and roots that I have learned? Do I spot them on billboards or signs, in newspapers and magazines?

Yes _____ No _____

3. Do I find them in other reading that I am doing? Do I *hear* them when other people say words in which they are used?

Yes _____ No _____

(This is one of the trickiest—and most helpful—tasks of all!)

4. Am I beginning to feel proud of my ability to know and use many word elements heretofore unknown to me?

Yes _____ No _____

If most of your answers are yes, then feel proud of your ability to take some new ideas, some new information and use it for your own gain. If your answers are mostly no, then maybe you might want to review the Learning Techniques involved in this text. Maybe you might want to examine your own goals: are you really interested in learning better ways to communicate with yourself and the world around you?

19. Without words, communications would be limited to shoves and grunts. But with the words you have here, thirty roots, thirty-two prefixes and many other words to learn, you can build thousands of words. With the Learning Techniques, you can conquer many tasks.

20. If you are doing well, *reward yourself.* Sit back and plan a party. Or do whatever it is that makes you happy.

21. If you are *not* doing very well, *reward yourself* by going back and reviewing, by picking up the tools behind you and *using* them for your own benefit.

22. Now try a new root, one that is used very often but that has several forms, so it may be a bit confusing. There are actually two roots:

DRC
sta

    sta—which means "to stand," as in stance and

    statu—which means "to stand erect" as in statue. Many other forms exist, for example:

    sti—constitution

    sis—insistence

    sto—restore

    sty—stylite

Perhaps you know the word constituents which refers to the voters in a particular area, the people who, possibly, "stand with" the lawmakers or Congressmen of that area.

23. Listed below are the prefixes you have had to date:

A-	_____	Inner-	_____
Ad-	_____	Inter-	_____
Auto-	_____	Intra-	_____
Bi-	_____	Mono-	_____
Com-	_____	Non-	_____
De-	_____	O-, Ob-	_____
Eu-	_____	Per-	_____
Ex-	_____	Poly-	_____
Hetero-	_____	Pre-	_____
Homo-	_____	Pro-	_____
Hyper-	_____	Re-	_____
Hypo-	_____	Sub-	_____
In-	_____	Trans-	_____
Il-	_____	Un-	_____

24. Fill in blanks with the meanings of each prefix. Refer to Data Retention Cards *only* if necessary.

Now, fit as many prefixes as you can on one of the three wheels below. Add any words using the roots *without* the prefixes: such as statutes, meaning "laws."

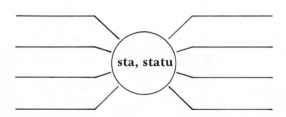

sta, statu

24. **NOTE:** Law comes from a term that has moved all around, in German, Old English, Dutch, Greek, Old Norse. Its meaning has remained fairly constant: "that which is set down." Comparison with a similar term, one you have already met, and one that comes almost directly from Latin and Greek, shows some interesting parallels:

Law or **leg:** to set down (from German, Old English Dutch, Greek, Old Norse)	**Leg:** to speak (from Latin, Greek) Also: **logos, logy**
Law	Legal
Lawyer	Legislature
Lay	Legacy
Ledge	Delegate
By-law	Logic
Outlaw	Prologue
Lair	Legitimate
	Legible
	Lecture

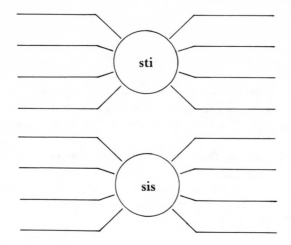

25. After you have recorded all the ones you can think of, check your answers with the wheels below.

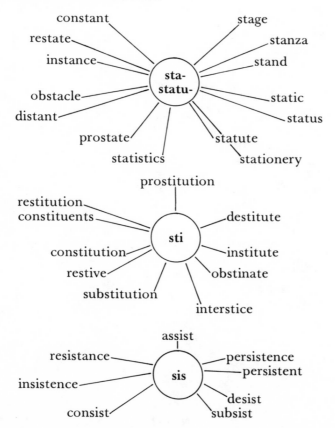

constant
restate
instance
obstacle
distant
prostate
statistics

sta-
statu-

stage
stanza
stand
static
status
statute
stationery

prostitution
restitution
constituents

sti

destitute
institute
obstinate
interstice

constitution
restive
substitution

assist
resistance
insistence

sis

persistence
persistent
desist
subsist

consist

27. **Sta**- also appears in stance, which refers both to the way one stands—physically—and to the stand one takes on topics—emotionally and intellectually. "The circumstances indicate that his stance is non-partisan."

1. **Circum**- means "surrounding." Circumlocution means talking in circles, around an idea. Circumnavigate means to "go around (navigate) the whole area."

2. Non-partisan means, simply, "not with any particular party."

Sti- appears in superstition. **Super**-, of course, means "huge"; it also means "over" or "above." Hopefully, we can "stand above" our superstitions.

Armistice is a curious word: It means a "stopping of arms"; arms refers to tools or weapons, armature.

26. That's thirty words—plus the ones in the notes—using one basic root and nine prefixes! *Many* more could be formed!

27. Many of these words are already known to you. Others you can figure out by knowing the prefix and root. Some you may need special help on. For example:

(A) Statute refers to "laws." Remember that **statu** is the root that means "to stand erect." Hopefully, our statutes "stand erect." Statutes are put together by legislative bodies of government; they differ from "common law."

(B) Restitution, the process of "restoring," means to return something or "to make up for loss or damage." It means literally "to set up" or "stand up again."

(C) Restive, on the other hand, means "restless, uneasy." It means literally "to stand back" or "stand away from."

(D) Destitute means "deserted" or "utterly without means." The root **statu** also means "to place" as well as "to stand erect." So to be destitute is "to have all things placed away."

(E) Likewise, desist links **de-** with the root, but in this instance, the root takes on the meaning of "to stand," so to desist is "to stand away from" or "to stop." **Cease and desist!**

(F) To subsist is "to barely make it." A subsistence allowance is an allowance that barely gives you enough to live on, to allow you to "remain standing."

28. Try linking the words on the left with the phrases on the right. *Do not* refer to the sentences above unless you absolutely *must.*

Statute _____   A. cut it out; don't do it.

Restitution _____   B. barely make it.

Restive _____   C. make amends for.

Destitute _____   D. laws set up by government bodies.

Desist _____   E. very, very poor.

Subsist _____   F. restless, uneasy.

Check your answers with answer key. If you missed any, go back and read the sentences above that dealt with the word you missed.

Answer Key
30. 1. asks
2. before
3. away
4. under
5. away

29. **Rog** comes from the root meaning "to ask," so interrogate literally means "to ask between." However, as we all know, an interrogation is a formal questioning, and sometimes the one who is being interrogated does not have much chance to exchange questions.

30. The root appears in other common words.

   1. You may recall the interrogative sentence, which is the sentence

      that _____ a question.

   2. Our **prerogatives** are the rights that we ask _____ all else. They are our privileges, that no one has the right to question.

   3. To **derogate** someone, on the other hand, is to detract from that

      person, to take _____ his good name. If you make **derogative** remarks about someone, you had better be sure of your prerogatives.

   4. **Surrogate** court is a kind of "under" court that takes care of wills, estates, among other things. Its development from **sub-**

      meaning_____ plus **rog** is not very clear.

   5. **Abrogate**, on the other hand, is to abolish someone's authority.

      To ask it _____, or annul it.

   Check your answers with the answer key. Hopefully, you will feel some rewards at knowing some terms that you may not have known before.

31. You should reward yourself by:

   (A) doing something you like to do after you have accomplished set goals;

   (B) experimenting with words;

   (C) avoiding those things which are neither fun nor helpful.

32. But how can you tell when something is either fun or helpful unless you try it? That's a problem!

33. Take suffixes, for example. Memorizing a list of meanings for twenty or thirty suffixes probably won't help you. But recognizing how suffixes change roots probably can increase your word knowledge.

34. Suffixes may not be as important as prefixes in helping you identify words, but they can be fun to experiment with. For example, you have seen the words:

communism	socialism	realism	**DRC**
idealism	Hinduism	Protestantism	-ism

But have you ever thought about the fact that **-ism** has a meaning all its own?

-ism: "doctrine or belief in."

So Communism, socialism and realism are all doctrines or beliefs in something. Stating just what each of these doctrines or beliefs consists of depends on one's own biases.

35. We make up new words easily by adding **-ism** to a root:

Mom-ism (from the early 1940s): The doctrine (or all powerfulness) of mom. How about popism? Dadism? Father-ism?

The only trouble with popism is that too many interpretations are possible. Belief in—father, a soft drink, some kind of music?

How about:

    deism: belief in God as the creator (but not the continuing director) of the universe (deus: God)

    sadism: from the Marquis de Sade—delight in cruelty

    puritanism: belief in pure moral code

36. What do we sometimes call the person who believes in these doctrines:

    A commun<u>ist</u>

    A social _____

    A real   _____

    A sad   _____

DRC
-ist

So the suffix **-ist** means: _____

Notice that some of the roots do not use this particular suffix. For example, one who believes in Protestantism is merely a Protestant. Same with Hindu. Buddhism, the belief, becomes Buddhist, the believer.

37. The suffix **-ant** as in Protestant (one who protests) also has a special meaning: one who believes or performs a certain way. We have: supplicant, applicant, militant and so on.

DRC
-ant

38. Here are some other common suffixes and some sample words (remember, the suffix always comes *after* the root):

Suffix	Meaning	Sample Word	
-able, -ible	capable of, able to	trainable, credible	*adjective*
-al	process, act of doing	revival, rehearsal	*adjective*
-ance, -ence	condition or quality of	credence, complaisance	*Noun*
-ate	to act or possess	create, substantiate	*verb*
-ful	have in abundance	plentiful, pitiful	
-itis	inflammation of	appendicitis	
-ize	to make similar to	lionize, subsidize	*Verb*
-ness	quality or condition	tiredness, flatness	
-ous	possessing, full of	contemptuous, outrageous	
-ship	status or function	scholarship, friendship	
-tion	act or process	deception, suction	*Noun*
-wise	position, or connection with	time-wise, space-wise	*adjective*

(A note of caution: some suffixes have meanings that differ slightly from the meanings listed above; **-ate**, for example, has special significance in chemistry. You would be wise to check your dictionary or glossary of chemical terms. Some suffixes are abused by being used too frequently and haphazardly: **-ize** and **-wise** are two good examples. Avoid them when possible, except in well-established words. Again, check your dictionary.)

39. As you look over the list, you will recognize many of the suffixes—without having been aware that you even knew them. Remember:

(A) Break words apart into manageable word elements—affixes and roots.

(B) Link the unknown to what you already know.

(C) Get feedback on whether your "knowns" are correct (make up Data Retention Cards for the suffixes *you* think are important).

(D) Practice them frequently—mull them, watch out for them while reading, listening, driving, walking, talking.

43. The suffix **-itis** is used in many terms referring to diseases:

laryngitis	neuritis	elephantitis
appendicitis	hepatitis	arthritis

You will find rewards in understanding new terms, in spelling them correctly and *using them easily!*

40. Now at this point, you can reward yourself by either:

    1. examining some of the suffixes in greater detail or

    2. by going on to paragraph 47.

    It's your decision. If you don't want to learn more suffixes, turn over to page 141. If you *do* want to learn more, continue with this page.

41. **-able:** We have used the words "manageable" and "recognizable" frequently in this text; they mean "capable of being managed" and "able to be recognized." So it is pretty easy to figure out that **-able**

    means: _____.

    DRC
    -able
    -ible

    The spelling gets tricky on this one. Sometimes it's **-ible**. Is there any pattern that you can see to addition of the suffix **-able** or **-ible**? When is a vowel dropped at the end of a root?

detestable	manageable	susceptible
debatable	forseeable	incredible
maintainable	agreeable	incorrigible

    Incorrigible is a curious term: means *not* capable of being corrected. **In-** (not), **corrig** (correct), **-ible** (capable of).

42. **-al:** means the act or process of doing, as in retrieval—the act of retrieving, bringing back (in order to keep the second syllable rhyming with "see," the *e* is kept here) and denial—the act of denying, rejecting.

    DRC
    -al

43. **-itis:** a suffix found especially in the health field, meaning "inflammation" as in bronchitis—inflammation of the bronchial tubes and bursitis—inflammation of a bursa; that is, of a knee, elbow or shoulder joint.

    DRC
    -itis

    There are six suffixes on the following page. Write the meaning and a sample word for each one.

    Check your answers with the answer key.

Answer Key

43.

Suffix	Meaning	Sample Word
-al	process, act of doing	proposal
-ant	one who acts	militant
-able	capable of, able to	suitable
-ism	belief in	idealism
-ist	one who believes	idealist
-itis	inflammation of	bronchitis

NOTE: You may wish to check your dictionary for any terms not listed above or in the preceding paragraphs on suffixes.

Suffix	Meaning	Sample Word
-al		
-ant		
-able, -ible		
-ism		
-ist		
-itis		

44. You may want to put more than just these six suffixes on Data Retention Cards. If you do, be sure you check your sample words with the dictionary. It is hard to go very far off on suffixes, but it is wise to spend a few minutes double-checking (getting *immediate feedback*) on what you are doing. If you find the suffixes helpful, *reward yourself,* do what you like to do or what you find helpful.

45. Check your DRCs and when you are ready, take the master test over the first six chapters. This includes all the prefixes and roots to date, so be sure you give yourself a fair shake by going over your DRCs.

46. If you do well, you may wish to file all your DRCs in an alphabetical card file. (A small, metal card box works very well.) You will add to your cards, hopefully, using words and phrases in the next chapters. But do not limit yourself to this text. Add words from all sources; check their meanings in your dictionary. Learn their pronunciations, their various meanings. Experiment with them.

47. From time to time, practice the prefixes and roots that you have on your DRCs. Chances are by now you have your reward: *word knowledge!* You can easily add to your foundation—now and for the rest of your life.

48. When you are ready, take the master quiz, which links prefixes, roots, and which asks you to remember only three suffixes: **-ism, -ist, -ant.** When you have completed the master quiz, check your responses with the response sheet on the following page.

Master Check-up Quiz: First Six Chapters

In the columns on the right, write the prefix and its meaning, the root and its meaning, and the suffix with its meaning.

Word	Prefix/meaning	Root/meaning	Suffix/meaning
1. supplicant			
2. agnosticism			
3. polygamist			

In the columns on the right, write the prefix and its meaning, and the root with its meaning.

Word	Prefix/meaning	Root/meaning
1. autograph		
2. eulogy		
3. induct		
4. confer		
5. intermit		
6. opponent		
7. transport		
8. ex-astronaut		
9. monologue		
10. prescribe		
11. retain		
12. reduce		
13. inverse		
14. aspect (ad-)		
15. incognito		

Give the meanings for the following terms.

1. **bio**

2. **cosmos**

3. **psych**

4. **theos**

Give the meanings for the following pairs.

1. **homo-**

   hetero-

2. **hypo-**

   hyper-

3. **inter**

   intra-

Check your responses with the following response sheet. Check any word elements that you missed; pull those cards out of the Data Retention Card file (or make up cards for any you don't have or don't know). Go over these carefully. Then take the tear-out quiz at the back of the book.

Master Check-up Quiz: First Six Chapters Completed

Word	Prefix/Meaning		Root/Meaning		Suffix/Meaning	
1. supplicant	**sub-**	under	**plic**	to fold	**-ant**	one who acts
2. agnosticism	**a-**	outside	**gnos**	knowledge	**-ism**	belief in
3. polygamist	**poly-**	many	**gamy**	marriage	**-ist**	one who believes

Word	Prefix/Meaning		Root	Meaning
1. autograph	**auto-**	self	**graph**	to write
2. eulogy	**eu-**	good	**log**	to study (to speak)
3. induct	**in-**	into	**duct**	to lead

	Word	Prefix/Meaning		Root	Meaning
4.	confer	**con-**	with	**fer**	to bear or carry
5.	intermit	**inter-**	between	**mit**	to send
6.	opponent	**ob-**	against	**pon**	to place
7.	transport	**trans-**	across	**port**	to carry
8.	ex-astronaut	**ex-**	outside of	**astro** (naut)	stars ship
9.	monologue	**mono-**	one	**log**	to study (speak)
10.	prescribe	**pre-**	before	**scrib**	to write
11.	retain	**re-**	back	**tain**	to hold
12.	reduce	**re-**	again	**duc**	to hold
13.	inverse	**in-**	into	**vers**	to turn
14.	aspect	**ad-**	to, toward	**spect**	to look
15.	incognito	**in-**	not	**gnos**	to know

	Term	Meaning
1.	**bio**	life
2.	**cosmos**	world, universe
3.	**psych**	mind, behavior
4.	**theos**	god or gods

	Word	Meaning
1.	**homo-**	the same
	hetero-	different
2.	**hypo**	under
	hyper	over, very
3.	**inter-**	between
	intra-	within

Chapter 7

Use the Best Tools Available

1. If you want to drive in a nail efficiently, use a sturdy hammer, not the heel of a shoe. If you want to get rid of the snow on your driveway, a big snow blower will work better than a snow shovel— but the snow shovel will do better than a whisk broom.

2. So it is with words and dictionaries. Some dictionaries are like whisk brooms—very useful for little jobs. The pocket size, paper back, for example. Portable as they are, they go along with a stack of school books, in a car pocket or on the bathroom shelf. They are cheap, usually seventy-five cents, so buy two or three. For spelling and synonym-type definitions, they are very useful.

3. For example: If you can't remember whether to write "a lot" and "all right" each as two words or each as one word, try finding them in your pocket dictionary. You won't, which means they are not *yet* acceptable in English as "alot" and "alright." (In larger dictionaries, "alright" is listed as a misspelling.)

4. But anyone interested in increasing word power should also have a desk-size dictionary. Some specific ones are recommended in paragraph 12.

5. Many good desk-size dictionaries are available. With from 150,000 to 250,000 separate entries (words with various classifying information), these books are *not* very portable. They can weigh four or five pounds. But the information included in them *is* portable—in your head—and can make word study easier and more fun.

6. A good desk-size dictionary costs under $10. In the average household, it should be replaced at least every ten years. That means for under one dollar a year, you have a good source not only for Scrabble games but also for increasing general intelligence.

7. For example: Let's say the management in your company has refused to accept **mediation** and you have been instructed to **boycott.**

7. **NOTE:** The plural of **medium** is **media** . . . as is the plural of **datum** is **data**.

You have heard of the new media and you know of multi-media (many media) devices for learning, including cassettes, tape recorders, film strips, TV. These are merely devices for getting knowledge or propaganda across to people—they are the "middle men" so to speak.

Are you familiar with a **medium**—a person who thinks he can communicate with the spirits of the dead, again a sort of "middle man."

What is the **medial** strip in four-land divided highways? Sure, the middle grassy or paved area.

Perhaps you know the word **median** in geometry and statistics. If not and you want to, look it up in your dictionary.

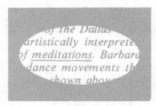

If you can rush home to your desk-size dictionary, you will find that mediation comes from the Latin word meaning "to be in the middle;" you already know the word "medium" or "average."

But you will also find that a more complex, formal stage of mediation, of settling differences between labor and management, is called **arbitration.**

8. So will you boycott? You can also discover from your dictionary that a land agent in Ireland 100 years ago refused to lower tenants' rents during very hard times; they, in turn, refused to have anything to do with him—they "boycotted" him. His name? Charles C. Boycott. Boycott, then, means to protest by refusing to have anything to do with something, such as refusing to buy products from a particular store or company because you don't like their beliefs or actions.

9. Or, for another example: Let's say you see the word **isometrics** in your morning newspaper. You can't get a handle on it through your knowledge of prefixes and roots—which should be the first source you check. So you turn to your dictionaries:

Pocket size dictionary: doesn't have **isometrics** listed. But you recognize the third and fourth syllables, **met-rics,** as close to meter. So you look up meter and find it means "measure" or "basic unit of length"—which you knew anyway. But still nothing on isometrics. So you turn to your desk-size dictionary. You find isometrics, but if your dictionary is very old, you won't find the definition you want. If it has been published within the past eight or ten years, you will probably find that isometrics refers to exercise involving equal contractions of muscles, **iso-** being the Greek word for "equal" or "homogeneous."

DRC
-iso

10. While you are thinking about **iso-** and **meter** you remember that you also saw the word **psychoanalysis.** So you run the same check again.

Pocket-size: a method of dealing with psychic disorders by study of the normally hidden content of the mind esp. (especially) to resolve conflict.

Desk-size: (1) The analytic technique originated by Sigmund Freud that uses free association, dream interpretation, and analysis of resistance and transference to investigate mental processes. (2) The theory of human psychology founded by Freud on the concepts of

11. **NOTE:** Two larger-than-desk-size dictionaries are these scholarly works which you might want to scan or study in your local library: *Webster's Third New International Dictionary,* and the *Oxford English Dictionary.* Webster's Third (the WNI) has 450,000 entries with many examples of how words are used in phrases and sentences. (The word itself is replaced by a ~ in these examples.)

The *Oxford English Dictionary* (the OED) has twelve volumes and two supplements, fourteen in all. The entry for "and" alone takes up four columns. You can discover such things as this: **xmas** was used as early as 1551; the *x* is the first letter of the Greek spelling of Christ. Many other dictionaries for studying words also exist: for slang, cliches, foreign words, difficult words, abbreviations, thesaurus (synonyms) and so on.

the unconscious, resistance, repression, sexuality, and the Oedipus complex. (3) Any psychiatric therapy incorporating such an analytic technique in such a theoretical framework.

11. If you want a brief, synonym-type definition, the pocket-size dictionary may serve your needs. When you want longer, more detailed information, the desk-size dictionary will answer some questions that the pocket-size will not. But when you want to see a word in context, see how it is used in phrases or sentences, or when you want to get a more thorough history of how the word has been used, then you may want to turn to a dictionary that is larger than the desk-size dictionaries: You will find these unabridged dictionaries in college classrooms or in your library. They can be very beneficial if you want detailed, special definitions, or rarely used words.

12. Back to desk-size dictionaries—some good ones are:

    American Heritage Dictionary of the English Language, American College Dictionary, Funk and Wagnalls Standard College Dictionary, Random House Dictionary of the English Language, Webster's New World Dictionary of the American Language, and *Webster's Seventh New Collegiate Dictionary.*

    Remember that dictionaries are sources for finding out how some experts say our language is being used, and has been used. Hundreds of scholars make up the dictionaries and millions of dollars go into producing them. But they are not flawless. Dictionaries are like freeways. By the time they are finished they are already out-of-date, because language changes constantly. Still, they happen to be one of the best sources most of us have for getting feedback (sometimes immediate) on word usage. However, do not take them as embodying static, unquestionable "truths."

13. You should also check the reference shelves of your library to get whatever helps you need from various specialized dictionaries, in psychology, social science, medicine, economics, just to name a few. Your librarian can help you with this. These special reference dictionaries—and your librarian—can save you a lot of time!

14. Remember to spend a few minutes familiarizing yourself with *any* dictionary you use. Look at the front pages; find out what is in the dictionary you have in your hands. Find out where the abbreviations are, where the pronunciation symbols are, what other aids

may be included. Then look at the back matter; find out what information is included *after* the alphabetical listings are completed. You may be surprised at the variety of helpful data that can answer questions and provide interesting scanning.

15. For example, if you have the *New Merriam-Webster Pocket Dictionary,* you will find that the back matter has a section of "New Words for a New Decade." And in that section you can find the word **isometrics** which you had judged as not included in pocket-size dictionaries. This one has it—along with a great deal (2800) of supplemental words, many of which have come into use only in the past few years.

16. So scanning the contents of your dictionary will not only help you learn more—but can also keep you from passing unfair judgment on a good tool for your use.

17. It is amazing how many people do not realize that several definitions exist for one word. If they stop to consider, they readily acknowledge that this is so. But they do not then go on to find out why the dictionary *they* use puts one meaning before another.

18. Take the word **bar,** for example. It has all kinds of meanings:

    1. a place one goes to drink
    2. a solid block of something: candy bar, soap bar
    3. a term having to do with lawyers—or barristers—and something vague about "passing their bar exams"
    4. a stretch of land, such as a "sand bar" or a "gravel bar"
    5. or in music: "play a few bars for me"

    All of these are nouns ("a bar," or "the bar") and form their plural by adding *s.* They all have qualities in common.

    But what about the verb: "to bar" someone?

    He will bar our admittance from the show.

19. Most words in English have more than one possible meaning. How do we tell which one we want when we consult a dictionary? How do the dictionary editors decide which meaning to put first? Is the dictionary definition always "correct?" Is it adequate for our purposes?

20. Different dictionaries list various definitions for the same word in different ways. When one word has several meanings, these mean-

ings must be listed in some order. Sometimes the oldest meaning for the word is given first. Sometimes the most common, or the central meaning for the word is given first. The first method is easier to determine than the second, as you can no doubt imagine. But the point is that *you* need to know how *your* dictionary lists definitions: oldest meaning first or most common meaning first.

21. Also, remember the point that was made in Chapter 1, paragraph 26: words mean different things to different people. Sometimes a dictionary definition does not tell you how a certain person is using a word.

22. Several types of definitions exist:

(A) Defining by using similar terms (synonyms) that may have slightly different interpretations: Synonyms *may* help shed some light on the term that needs defining, but generally they are about as vague as the term itself. For instance, read this dialogue:

Sue: That was preordained.
Rose: What do you mean, "preordained?"
Sue: Oh, you know—predestined.
Rose: Oh.

(B) Defining by using opposite words (antonyms): Again, the same vagueness may plague you. Consider this dialogue:

Pete: That's very ambiguous.
Joe: What does "ambiguous" mean?
Pete: Well, it's the opposite of lucid.
Joe: Oh.

(C) Defining by example: Although this may help clarify the meaning of the word, more than by merely giving synonyms or antonyms, it has some special dangers. One example does *not* make a case. Let's say that someone says to you:

"Hey, that community house is a real haven."

You ask that person what he means by a "haven" and he says:

"Go there any morning and you can get free coffee and doughnuts."

Well, you go there some morning at 11:59; you are *very* hungry, you find the place closed. You may not think it much of a "haven."

(D) Defining by operation: Sometimes the only way to figure out whether people are defining words in similar ways is to ask them, "How does that word operate?" That is, who is doing what, when, where, and sometimes why. It asks for extended examples, not just one. If someone tells you he believes in "law and order" or "equal education" or "freedom of worship," before you agree or disagree with him, you had better figure out how he is using the terms. About whom is he speaking? What are the people doing? When? Where? What happens? What are they after? It is an endless task. But it is an essential one if communication is to take place. Sometimes the dictionary just isn't adequate for defining terms. For example, you ask yourself: What is a good teacher? Your dictionary won't tell you. You have to figure out how a good teacher *operates*. So much for the difficulties in definitions.

23. Another good source of word power can come from professionals and technicians speaking *in their field of knowledge.* For example, a teacher or professor should know about various educational degrees. Maybe you have always wondered what Ph.D. means or D.D. or A.A.S. And you've wondered about the Doctor on the faculty who is surely not connected with medicine. Well, a teacher or professor can tell you that:

Ph.D. stands for Doctor of Philosophy and is the oldest doctoral degree there is. You can become a Ph.D. in psychology, in English, in mathematics, in sociology and so on.

Ed.D. stands for Doctor of Education

D.D. stands for Doctor of Divinity

All of these are doctors in fields *outside* of medicine. In medicine you can get such degrees as:

D.D.S.—Doctor of Dental Surgery

M.D.—Doctor of Medicine

D.O.—Doctor of Osteopathy

There are other doctorates, such as J.D., Doctor of Jurisprudence. Most of these take at least seven or eight years of study after high school.

24. Then there are Masters Degrees (M.A., Master of Arts; M.S., Master of Science). And Bachelors Degrees. Do you know what their abbreviations stand for?

A B.A. degree means _____.

A B.S. degree means _____.

You may also be familiar with the two-year degrees, requiring about sixty hours of course work in college. These are called Associate Degrees. Besides the A.A. and the A.S., we also have in some colleges the A.A S., Associate in Applied Science.

25. Now try filling in the blanks in the following grid of degrees: You should be able to fill in all fourteen missing areas from information you had or have just read.

Degrees	Abbreviation	Stands for	Approximate years after high school	Total semester hours
Associates	A.A.	Associate of Arts	2 years (15 hours per semester) (no summer school)	60 hours
	_____	Associate of Science		
	A.A.S.	_____ of Applied _____		
Bachelors	B.A.	Bachelor of _____	4 years (16 hours per semester no summer school)	138 semester hours
	B.S.	_____ _ _____		
Masters	_____	Master of Arts	5-6 years	150 semester hours— at least
	_____	_____ of Science		
	M.S.W.	_____ of Social Work		
Doctorates	D.D.S.	_____ _ _____	7-9 years	200 semester hours
	Ed.D.	_____ of Education		
	J.D.	Doctor of _____		
	D.O.	_____ of Osteopathy		
	_____	Doctor of Medicine		
	Ph.D.	_____ of Philosophy		

26. A teacher can also tell you, if you don't know already, that "hours" in college traditionally has meant the number of hours actually spent in class each week. That is, a three hour English class will meet three times a week for one semester; on the other hand, a five hour biology class might meet at least five times a week, plus two or three additional hours in the laboratory, for one semester. For each class you pass, you receive so many hours credit, like credits in a bank toward graduation.

27. The same goes for medical and legal terms; experts working in those areas can give us a lot of help on how terms are used. Some medical and legal terms should be known by all educated laymen. We all may serve on juries. We may read about **extradition** or **habeas corpus** in the newspapers. Besides, lawyers tell us that if everyone were more careful about how words are used, they wouldn't have as much business. That is, a lot of lawsuits arise simply because the parties did not know or did not agree on the definitions of various terms.

28. Remember the earlier caution when you turn to experts for definitions of words: words mean different things to different people, even sometimes to those in the same profession.

29. Another important source of word knowledge is from your reading of texts and other materials. For example, in just this chapter you have come across these words:

> synonym: paragraph 2
> portable: paragraph 2
> mediation: paragraph 7
> boycott: paragraph 7

Two had been used earlier; two had not. Did you read the notes on the opposite page for **portable** and **mediation**? Did you try to figure out from the context what **synonym** meant if you did not already know?

Spending a little time mulling over words, relishing them, using them, can help make them a part of you.

30. Take synonym. Does it mean:

_____ a word that means about the same as another word (happy, glad)

_____ a word that sounds the same as another word (bare, bear)

_____ a word that is the opposite of another word (introvert, extrovert)

The first one is right. Can you think of a word that begins **syn-**? Just by experimenting with this one word "synonym," you can link lots of other words and learn some new ones. Can you pull any other possibilities out of synonym? What is the root? Well, it is **nym** (or **onym**). Our word "name" comes from **nym**—note it is the root in:

> homo**nym** (words or names that sound alike)
>
> anto**nym** (words or names that are opposites)

Homo- is a prefix you have already had. Check your DRCs in case you have forgotten it. **Ant-** is not only a bug but also a prefix; what does **anti**-war mean? _____ Against war, so **anti-** or **ant-** means "against" or the "opposite of."

31. Now test yourself on these three by labelling the following pairs of words either: synonym, antonym, or homonym. Remember: There are no such things as *exact* opposites or likenesses, so you have to be flexible.

    hot—cold _____

    force—violence _____

    bear—bare _____

    glory—praise _____

    blue—blew _____

    stingy—giving _____

    Check your responses with the answer key on the following left-hand page.

32. **Nym** is a root meaning (a) _____ . What does the Greek prefix **syn-** mean? It's like the Latin prefix, **com-**, which means (b) _____ . So synonym is literally "named with" or "similar." What other words do you know that begin with **syn-** or **sym-**? (c.) _____ How about sympathy. Do you know the word **pathos**? It generally means "pity" or "compassion." It once meant "sickness." Can you think of other words using pathos? How about empathy, "to have shared feelings"; pathetic, "to really feel something is pitiful."

33. Being able to identify the meanings of word elements, whether they are affixes or roots, is, of course, vital to understanding. But being able to recognize these elements in *new* words is also important—even though they may not unlock complete understanding of the

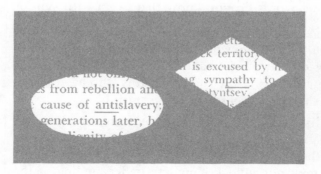

Answer Key

31. antonyms
    synonyms
    homonyms
    synonyms
    homonyms
    antonyms

32. (a) name
    (b) with
    (c) synthetic, synthesis, symphony, symposium

new word. So try identifying the word elements of words given in this chapter and other chapters.

34. For example, you know the term **isometrics**. If you were given the following pairs:

isometrics   isotope

systems analysis   metric system

you could point to the similarities in the word elements, like this:

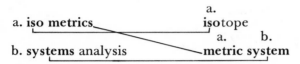

35. Or try another:

a. systems analysis   isolate

b. relate   retrieval system

The word elements **system**, **re-**, and **late** were used in both columns.

36. There are two sets of words below and on the following page, eight lines on each. See how quickly you can underline same word elements in different columns and put identifying letters (a, b, c . . .) over word elements in column 2, as above. Some part of each word from list on the left should be used.

a. portable   arbitrary decision

b. synonym   credentials

c. entries   anonymous

d. mediation   mediator

e. boycott   import

f. arbitration   disembody

g. embodying   reentry

h. credit hours   Charles C. Boycott

37. Go over your list carefully; some part of each word from the column on the left can be found in the column on the right. Now try another list, this time with words from this and other chapters:

a. extradition   antipathy

b. pathos   cosmopolitan

c. aversion   homosexual

d. empathy   expedition

e. cosmos   order of execution

f. homonym   pathetic fallacy

g. inordinately

h. antonym

38. This time did you find some part of each word from the column on the left in the column on the right? You should have. **Antipathy,** for example, has parts of **antonym** and **pathos.** Do you remember what **anti-** means?_____ How about **pathos?** _____ . If someone has an **antipathy** for another person, is the feeling one of liking or disliking? _____ . (**Anti-** means "against"; **pathos** means "feeling.")

39. This may seem fairly simple, but you will be amazed how helpful it is, once you are on the look out for the word elements you already know in words that are unfamiliar.

40. When you look for and recognize word elements that you know within words that you are not quite sure about, you are using the best tool you have: your own head. It is the *sine qua non* of word study:

> **sine qua non** (sin-i kwa non)—without that nothing

Without your own good head, using it, that is, to *think* with, word study doesn't go very far.

As you mull over words, using your texts and other printed matter as resources for word study, you are using your best resources:

Your own senses.

41. In Chapter 1, you were advised to read words aloud, to pronounce them, roll them around in your mouth and thus in your head. Then you were advised to write them, to put them down where you can see them and work with them. By this time you are using:

Auditory sense—hearing words

Kinetic sense—writing words, moving the hands

Visual sense—looking at words

42. Other senses—there are many more than five—can come into vocabulary growth: senses of joy, pain, weariness, hunger. To some people, thinking is the antithesis or opposite of the senses, the feelings. They are guilty of splitting man—your senses are *part* of your thinking. If you will use this kind of master sense to direct and be consciously aware of the other senses, you can go far. Can't you *feel* it: your heart beat a little faster, your posture a little more erect; if you look in the mirror, you'll see that your pupils are a little larger—you see, you are thinking!

43. Now use this marvelous thinking state to take the following quiz:

1. At the beginning of Chapter 3 you were asked to fill in a word-wheel using the root **port**, as in import, export, report, and so

   on. **Port** means _____ so a **portage**

   would be _____ing boats and packs overland on a canoe trip.

2. Synonym, antonym and homonym have what root in common:

   _____ which means: _____. Now link the following words with the appropriate meanings:

   _____ synonyms   A. having similar meanings

   _____ antonyms   B. having opposite meanings

   _____ homonyms   C. sound alike

3. Mediation has the root _____ in it, which means

   _____ as in mediator, medial strip and _____

   _____ .

4. If you boycott your local super market, what do you do?

   _____.

Answer Key

1. to carry, carry(ing)
2. **nym**—name
   A. synonyms
   B. antonyms
   C. homonyms
3. media—middle, medium/median/
   immediate/mediocrity . . .
4. refuse to make purchases
5. (b)
6. yes
7. hours earned in college that are "credited" toward graduation
8. to
9. de
10. surrender to the outside
11. have the body
12. **path**—feeling; illness or suffering

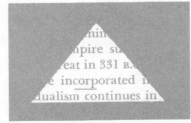

N—160

5. Arbitration involves which of the following processes:

   (a.) _____ standing in a grape arbor

   (b.) _____ management and labor representatives discussing differences—usually through a mediator

   (c.) _____ stating that your side is right and the other side absolutely wrong

6. To be disembodied could mean to free the soul from the body.

      Yes _____ No _____

7. "Credit hours" refers to:

   _____ the time you spend in line paying off your bills

   _____ the hours before and after work

   _____ if neither of these, then what?

8. **Ad valorem** taxes are taxes paid according ___ the **value** of your
                                    ad-
property or belongings.

9. **Jurisdiction** means the word—or application—of the law. Juris, you will recognize in the word jury. "By the law" is called **de jure**; the antonym of this, "by the fact" is _____ facto.

10. The word **tradition** comes from the Latin word meaning "a surrendering." You can figure out what **extradition** refers to since you know **tradition** in Latin meant surrendering and extra-marital means outside of marriage, extraordinary means outside of the ordinary.

Extradition means _____ to the _____—or more specifically, giving up for trial in another state or country (outside) a person who has been accused of some crime. **Extra-** means outside of—just like **ex-**.

DRC
extra-

11. **Corpus** means "body" as in Marine Corps, corps de ballet. Habe-as is the Latin word for "have." Habeas corpus means, literally,

DRC
corps

_____ _____ _____. How do you suppose this differs from extradition?

12. Sympathy, empathy, antipathy, pathos are all nouns using the

root _____ which means _____ .

44. **NOTE:** If you are a mystery magazine buff, you have perhaps run into the term *corpus delecti,* which refers to the body of the victim in a murder case. *Delecti* comes from a word meaning "to entice away" and appears in other, rather different terms: *delicacy, delicatessen,* and *delicious!*

It once meant, and still does in medical terminology, _____

_____ , as in pathology.

Check your answers with the answer key on page N—160.

Record below any word elements with which you had trouble, give their meanings, and use them in a sample word.

Word Elements	Meaning	Sample Word

44. Now expand the three roots **nym,** **path,** and **corps** into word wheels, using as many prefixes, suffixes, and additional roots as you can think of.

    Refer to the master lists of prefixes, roots and suffixes in paragraph only if necessary!

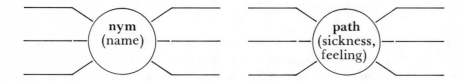

You know that the word **habeas corpus** means "to have the body." How many words can you form using the root **corps**?

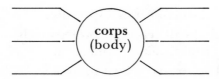

Check your word wheels with the ones below once you have added as many word elements to the roots as you can.

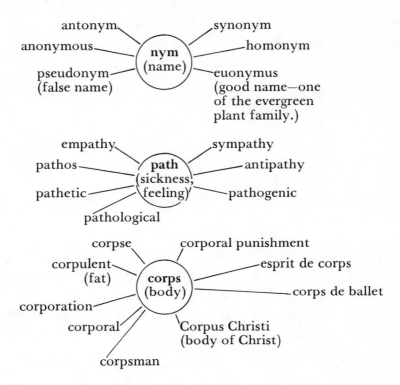

Again, you have been able to form perhaps two dozen words from just the three roots: **nym, path** and **corps.** Remember that the word *corps* is pronounced *without* the *p* or *s;* sounding as if it were *core.* We do say *corpse* sounding the *p* and *s;* the *e* on the end so indicates. But we say *core*-duh-ballay (corps de ballet).

45. So you have a variety of excellent tools for expanding your word power:

1. Resource material—dictionaries, especially.

2. Experts—in their field—teachers, professionals and technicians of various sorts; cooks, painters and so on.

3. Your own good senses—your own good brain.

Brains are marvelous things. They can be used to open all sorts of doors—both literally and metaphorically. You can push some doors open with your head, if they aren't latched too tight. But you can also open lots of doors with your thinking power, by "using your head." Maybe you can't become the King or Queen of England. But maybe you can become President of the United States, or Premier of Canada. Whatever it is you want to do, take the best you can get from others, master-mind your own senses, and use your head.

In Chapter 7 you have learned some new roots and prefixes:

Prefixes	Roots
Anti-	**Juris**
Extra-	**Media**
Iso-	**Metric**
Syn-	

and you have run into some terms that have fairly specialized meanings:

boycott
arbitration
sine qua non
ad valorem

The last two have decidedly foreign airs.

You have also learned or been reminded of the various kinds of degrees, including a variety of doctorates. You have learned about dictionaries and definitions, about using experts and texts as sources for learning new words or for clarifying meanings of old ones. And you, most of all, have been encouraged to rely on your own good senses. Don't cheat yourself. Use the best tools available.

When you are ready, take the quiz on tear-out sheets at the back of the book.

2. **NOTE:** Geriatrics has become an increasingly important field with the growth in the number of aged in America. Geriatrics refers especially to the medical study of the aged; gerentology to more general needs of the aged.

4. **NOTE:** Increase, increment—both grew out of the same root, but increment refers to small changes in one direction or another, to both increases and decreases.

7. **NOTE:** Is heretic a word you use? Referring to someone who doesn't buy the usual or "accepted" beliefs? Heretic and its sister word heresy, have nothing to do with heredity. You have nothing to say about your heredity; you are heir to that. But you can determine your own heresies (dissents).

Chapter 8

Study the Things You are Most Interested in First—

Have a Reason for Learning

1. A good way to figure out what you want to do with your life is to take a look at what you do with your spare time. Do you like to read? Talk with friends? Work on machines? Sew? Cook? Draw?

2. If you think you want to be an architect, but you hate to work with pen and paper, forget it. If you want to be a teacher but can't stand kids, go into gerentology. ("Gera"—old age; gerentology—study of the aging.)

3. If you are absolutely convinced that you can't learn a new language at twenty or sixty years of age, chances are you can't. (If you think you can, you no doubt can. Age doesn't have nearly as much to do with it as what's in your head.)

4. The point is that you learn best the things you are interested in learning. You learn best what you like or what you need to know for vocational, social or other reasons. Our emotions can play a pretty strong part in the learning process. If we think we can learn, if we want to learn, and if what is to be learned is handed to us in sufficiently small increments, then we can grasp it.

5. That last step is important. In order to attempt the job before us, we have to be able to do the preceding steps. Then we can tackle the one at hand.

6. So learn what *you* want to learn *when* you are ready to learn it! And know you *can* learn it.

7. One of the problems about picking a field to learn is that the "fields" of learning are not well defined. For example, let's say you want to learn terms that apply to the field of anthropology or the social sciences in general. You have seen the word "indigenous," let's say, and you want to know what it means. So you look it up and you check its root: Indigenous: four syllables: in-dig-e-nous. Means "native" or born in the area." "The American Indian is

indigenous in the U.S." And you find that the root is **gene** which means "a unit of heredity"—or transmission from one **gene**ration to the next. But look what else you can do with that root:

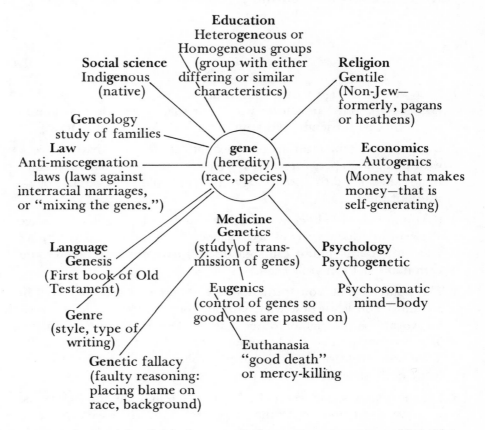

8. You have eight fields here—and there are more—that employ the root **gene** in some way or other. Some of the terms are not exclusively used within the field named above; for example, heterogeneous and homogeneous are certainly terms that are used outside the field of education.

9. You can also spin off from these words; you can identify elements that are used in other words, as **eu-** and **psycho** above. The game is almost endless!

10. However, it is possible to classify certain terms and meanings as especially belonging to certain fields. From the fields touched upon

in this chapter, you should pick those that interest you most and study those *first*. You may not wish to study or read the other sections at all.

11. On the following pages are terms that are used commonly in these fields:

Following these are two groups of words and phrases:

12. If you wish to study business and legal terms first, begin at the bottom of this page.

13. If you wish to skip the business and legal terms and start with another section, turn to the page designated above for the section you want to study, and begin working on that page. Begin where *you* want to begin. Make up Data Retention Cards as you go along but *only for those words or phrases that you want* to retain. Check-up quizzes occur at the end of each section within the chapter. You may wish to skip around in the chapter. But above all, study first what you want to learn—or have a reason for learning.

Business and Legal Terms

14. Have you seen the term acquitted in the newspaper and wondered if the person who was "acquitted" was found guilty or innocent? You now have the skills from this text to break the word apart:

ac- (ad- meaning "to, toward") + **quit** (meaning "stop" or "rest")

so you can figure out that acquitted means "to put to rest," or "to set free." "To quiet" someone, so to speak, by releasing or discharging him. This is only one of many legal terms that the layman should know.

15. But ask a lawyer how many people make mistakes in business transactions simply because they do not understand the terms. She or he

16. **NOTE:** Cantor, one who sings in the religious services at a synogogue, may sing or chant the words of the service. **Cant, chant** comes from a Latin word *carmen* meaning song. (Are you familiar with Bizet's opera "Carmen?" A **chan**teuse, a modern songstress, and a **char**mer, one who charms, also come from the root meaning "song.")

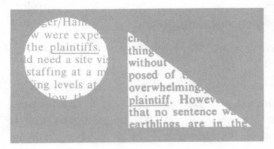

will probably tell you "quite a few!" Some people have trouble distinguishing between:

(A) The lessor and the lessee

(B) The plaintiff and the defendant

(C) Real property and personal property

If they would link these terms to things they already know—a technique you have mastered in using this book—they might save themselves both time and money.

16. (A) For example, in lessor and lessee, only the suffixes differ. The suffix **-or** as in lessor appears in many English words:

suitor	cantor	tutor
mentor	speculator	doctor

and means "one who *performs* the action." The lessor is leasing his property to the lessee. The suffix **-ee** also appears in other English words:

addressee	employee	referee

and simply means "one who *receives* the action." With this in mind, it becomes clear that:

a mortgagor is one who _____

a mortgagee is one who _____

17. (B) Similarly, by linking unknowns with already knowns, you can clarify any uncertainty about:

plaintiff—one who is complaining, who files a suit against someone

defendant—one who is defending, who has the suit brought against him

When a woman sues a man for a divorce, she is called plaintiff _____ or defendant _____? If someone has been charged with a crime and that person is appearing in court to stand trail, that person is the defendant _____ or the plaintiff _____?

The defendant *defends* himself against charges brought by the one who is complaining, or the plaintiff.

18. (C) What is the difference between real and personal property. Well, more than 300 years ago, a distinction was made between property that was immovable (real) and property that one could carry around (personal). So real property means real estate, land, or buildings. Personal property is the items you can take with you—from the piano to the wristwatch.

    Is your car real or personal property? You can't exactly carry it around. But neither is it "immovable." So automobiles fall under the "personal property" label.

19. Now mark true (T) or false (F) after each of the following statements:

    _____ 1. The lessor is one who is leasing (renting over a set period of time) his property.

    _____ 2. The lessee is the one who receives the lease, who lives in the property for a set period of time.

    _____ 3. A mortgagor is one who mortgages his property.

    _____ 4. A mortgagee is the one who receives the mortgage—and gives the mortgagor a certain sum of money, knowing that if the mortgagee cannot repay the money, the property can be taken over by the mortgagor.

    _____ 5. The plaintiff is the one who complains and files suit against someone.

    _____ 6. The defendant is the one who has charges made against him.

    _____ 7. Real property is "immovable" property, such as land, buildings, houses, commonly called "real estate."

    _____ 8. Personal property is the stuff one can move.

20. They were all true. You can get the idea that linking things you already know—prefixes, roots, suffixes—to new terms can help you in learning words in a special field.

21. The same goes for words in legal and business terminology that are written like foreign words. For example:

(A) ad valorem

(B) habeas corpus

(C) ad hoc

(D) de jure

(E) de facto

You learned earlier that:

1.   the prefix **ad-** meaning "to" or "towards"
2.   the prefix **de-** meaning "down" or "away from"
3.   the word **corpus** meaning "body"

So you are already on your way.

22. (A) In ad valorem you can recognize not only the prefix **ad-** but also the root **value** (valor—value). So ad valorem means "according *to* the *value.*" That one is easy: "according to the value." But according to the value of what? Well, supposedly, your ad valorem taxes are decided "according to the value" of the things you own.

23. (B) Take a look at the next word—habeas corpus. Corpus means "body." How about habeas? Our word *have* comes from habeas. So habeas corpus means "to have the body." The writ of habeas corpus

then means a written order to _____ or bring a person before a judge for trial.

24. (C) The **ad-** in ad valorem means "to" or "according to." In ad hoc, **ad-** means "to" and **hoc** means "this." The meaning goes beyond this, however. An ad hoc committee is one that is put together *to* meet *this* special occasion. If we were to form a committee to plan a party, and if the committee would no longer function after the party, then we would have an ad hoc committee—formed to meet this special occasion.

25. (D, E) De jure and de facto are simple. Especially if we are flexible in their interpretation. **Jure** you can recognize as being a part of jury, jurisdiction, jurisprudence. **Facto,** of course, is the same root as "fact."

> de jure means "by law"
>
> de facto means "in fact"

A married couple who are separated—living apart—but not divorced

would be separated de facto _____ or de jure _____? (check one)

27. **NOTE:** You have heard people say: "I was absolutely mortified." Well, surely they were using the words metaphorically; they were not *really* "caused to die." That is another one of these hyperboles discussed earlier!

They are not yet separated by law (divorce) so they have a **de facto** separation.

26. So you have pairs of words which are easier to remember than singles because you can pit one against the other. You can also build mnemonic devices for keeping them in your usage. Refer to the paragraphs where these pairs were dealt with if you have trouble remembering what they mean.

	Paragraph
plaintiff, defendant	17
real property, personal property	18
de facto, de jure	25
lessor, lessee	16
mortgagor, mortgagee	16

To these you can link other terms; for example:

grantor, grantee _____

The grantor is the one who _____ and the

grantee is the one who _____.

Did you write "one who grants" or "one who makes a grant" for grantor, and "one who receives the grant" for grantee? You also have terms employing word elements already known to you, such as:

ad hoc (**ad** being a prefix meaning _____)

habeas corpus (corps being a root meaning _____)

27. These can all be expanded by adding other terms, within and without the legal and business fields. For example, the terms mortgage links the root **mort** meaning "death" with the root **gage** meaning "pledge." We mortals use the root **mort** in many words. How many can you think of:

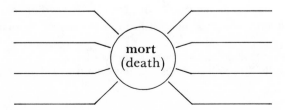

29. **NOTE:** Confidence: with faith. Now check such terms as:

Infidel: not having faith (of *the* faith, whether it is Christian, or Moslem)
Infidelity: not being faithful
Diffidence: away from faith—in oneself; diffidence evidences
itself in both shyness and distrust. (**Dis-** plus **fid**el)
Fidelity: devotion, constancy; do you know Beethoven's opera "Fidelio,"
about the wife who was so devoted that she saved her husband's life?

NOTE on a **NOTE:** Do you know that wife means, and probably comes from the same root as woman—both leaning on the term man (which meant person). Female, also, has a male term in it. But female comes from "one who suckels," and is linked with fetus, the unborn form in the womb. From fetus come such words as:

effeminate—meaning "out of woman," or weak.
effete—literally, "out of the fetus" or unproductive, self-absorbed.

Check your word wheel with the one below, filling in words that may not have occurred to you on the first go-around. Did you add as many prefixes as you could? For example, how do you link the prefix **in-** to **mort**al?

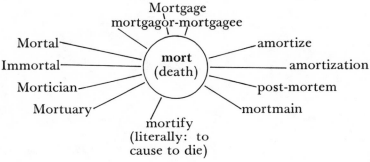

Mortgage
mortgagor-mortgagee

Mortal

Immortal

Mortician

Mortuary

mort
(death)

amortize

amortization

post-mortem

mortmain

mortify
(literally: to
cause to die)

28. Some help in spelling is again possible by recognizing that mortgage—pronounced without the *t*—comes from the word **mort** and still includes the *t* in the spelling. Some of the words may not be at all familiar; for example:

> mortmain: literally "dead-hand," referring to institutional ownership of property which cannot be transferred.

> amortize: literally "to deaden," referring to getting rid of debts. In accounting practice, amortization means to write off an expenditure over a period of time.

29. The latter word, amortize, you will probably see far more often than the first one: mortmain. But the point is that no matter what words you run into in the business-legal world, chances are you can:

> 1. recognize some word elements that are familiar to you
> 2. thereby linking the unknown to the known.

If you then

> 3. get immediate feedback

either from your dictionary, your textbook, or from experts in the field—and then:

> 4. add Data Retention Cards to your file
> 5. and practice those words you want to know.

You will then have these new business and legal terms under control. You can then use them appropriately, with confidence.

Answer Key

30. 1. **-or:** one who performs the act
        -ee: one who receives the action

   -or: **-ee:**
   suitor   respondee
   mentor   addressee
   cantor   employee
   tutor   referee
   speculator

   2. cannot
   3. plaintiff
   4. de jure or de facto
   5. **mort**—death

30. Now try a check-up quiz over the words in this section.

    1. The suffixes **-or** and **-ee** have been used in this section. Give their meaning and use them in three pairs of words:

    -or means _____ **-ee** means _____

Sample Words:

    1.

    2.

    3.

    2. Real property is distinguished from personal property in that real property can _____ cannot _____ be moved.

    3. If you sue your landlord because he did not perform some service he said he would perform, you will be termed in court the plaintiff_____ or the defendant_____?

    4. "Women have equal rights." Is that a de facto statement_____, a de jure statement _____?

    5. Mortician, post-mortem, mortals, mortify—all these words have in common the root _____ meaning _____ _____.

31. Question 4 was loaded. Women *do* have equal rights by law (de jure) in most areas of the United States. But having equal rights in fact (de facto) is a question you will have to answer on your own. The others you can check with the answer key.

32. You will probably be amazed at how many business and legal terms you can identify now that you know a sizeable number of Latin and Greek word elements. Using the skills you have learned in this text will aid you in learning more business and legal terms efficiently and effectively.

Health Related Terms

33. Without meaning to confuse the patient, a physician may sometimes use terms familiar to him but unfamiliar to his client.

34. For example, the physician may speak of cardiac arrest. Cardiac is the Greek word for "heart," so:

    cardiac arrest means "stopping the heart"

35. As pointed out in the introduction to this book, many scientific and literary terms come from old Greek roots. Sometimes English users put them together in ways not used by the Greeks, but the roots themselves have stayed fairly free of change for the last 2,000 years. For instance:

Root	English translation
Cardio	heart
Cephalo	head
Chromo	color
Derm	skin
Hema, hemo	blood
Hydr, hydro	water
Osteo	bone
Path	feeling, suffering, disease
Pneum	wind, air
Pod, poda, ped	foot
Soma	body
Thermo	heat

36. Some of these you can link fairly easily with terms you already know:

    Pneum—(as in pneumonia, a disease of the lungs)

    Derm—as in hypodermic, the name of a needle that goes under the skin

    Cardio—you noted above, means _____ , as in cardiac arrest, cardiograph, cardiology

    Hydr—as in hydrant, hydrogen, hydrochloric acid

    Thermo—as in thermometer, thermostat

    So it is easy to figure out that: (match the two columns)

    pneum _____ water

    derm _____ heat

    cardio _____ skin

    hydro _____ heart

    thermo _____ air, wind

37. Some roots can be linked to each other to form new words:

    1. **Cephalic** and **hydro** are linked to form hydrocephalic or
    _____ —more specifically cerebrospinal
    (brain-spine) fluid—in the head.

    2. **Osteo** and **path** are linked to form osteopath or literally bone
    disease; however, an osteopath is a kind of physician who treats
    more than diseases of the bone.

    3. You have no doubt heard of chromosomes. Scientists can easily
    color these little bodies (**somes**) with dye, hence they were
    called chromosomes or colored bodies, **chrom** being a word for
    "color." It may also be useful to remember that among other
    things chromosomes transmit such things as hair, eye and skin

    color. **Chromo** means _____ and **soma** means _____ .

38. Some of the roots do not appear frequently outside the field of
medicine. For example: **hemo** occurs in the well-known medical

terms: hemorrhage (to discharge large amounts of _____) and

in hemorrhoid (a swollen vessel which contains _____).
But its other uses are less well-known to laymen.

For most of us, the standard, desk-size dictionaries, such as those
listed in Chapter 6, offer adequate descriptions of these and other
medical terms. We may look them up if we, or someone we know, is
labeled with a specific medical term. Let's say we hear of someone
having cerebral palsy. We can look it up and discover that cerebral
refers to the brain and palsy means "weakened" or "impaired."
Then we can link:

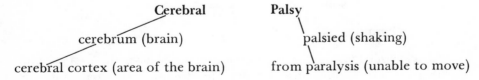

Anyone wishing more technical information about medical terms
can consult one of the good medical dictionaries to be found on the
reference shelves in libraries or in book stores.

39. One term from the list at the beginning of this section appears very
frequently in non-medical terminology. That word is **pod**, or **poda**—
also written **ped**. It appears in such words as:

Podiatrist: one who treats _____ailments.

Podium: a raised platform for one to put his _____ on.

Pedestrian: one who travels on _____ .

Also in impediment, impede, pedal, expedition, expedite, pedigree. A foot-warmer could be called a thermo-ped!

40. All twelve of these terms can be linked with word elements that you have learned earlier in this book. Before attempting some of these, give yourself a check-up quiz to see how many of the medical terms you now know.

Fill in blank with meaning of roots listed below:

cardio   _____

cephalo   _____

chromo   _____

derm   _____

hema, hemo   _____

hydr, hydro   _____

osteo   _____

path   _____

pneum   _____

pod, poda   _____

somato, soma   _____

thermo   _____

Check your meanings with the meanings given on the first page of this section. If you missed any, refer to the earlier paragraphs in which the root was described. Then write a word using that root next to your corrected meaning in space to right of the word you missed.

41. Now try the following quiz to see how well you can apply these medical roots in a variety of words and phrases.

1. Several of these roots are commonly linked with the word **logy**, meaning "the study of":

   A. The study of the heart is called _____ logy.

   B. The study of the skin is called _____ atology.

   C. The study of disease is called _____ ology.

2. **Graph**, meaning "writing" or "recording of," and **meter**, meaning "measurement," are both linked with some of these words. Fill in the blanks below by giving the meanings of the terms listed:

   Pedometer means _____

   Cardiograph means _____

   Thermometer means _____

3. In the first chapter you had a word **psych** meaning "mind" or "behavior." Try linking it with: **path** to form a word meaning

   "a mind that is suffering"_____ (referring to a per-
   ‎   (mind + suffering)

   son who operates outside of normal patterns). Link **psych** with

   soma to form a word meaning "mind-body" functions: _____
   ‎   (mind +

   ____ ic.
   body)

4. If someone loses excessive water from his body, (one might say

   that the *water* moves *away* from his body), then he is _____
   ‎   (down,

   _____ ated.
   away — water)

5. A drill that is run by using compressed *air* is called a _____-

   atic drill.

6. You could make up a word for someone having a many-colored

   head: a _____-_____-_____ .
   ‎   (many colored head)

Answer Key

1. A. cardiology
   B. dermatology
   C. pathology
2. Pedometer measures steps taken.
   Cardiograph records heart movements.
   Thermometer measures heat or temperature.
3. psychopath, psychosomatic
4. dehydrated
5. pneumatic
6. polychromachephalous
7. blood, head
8. heart vessel

7. A cerebral hemorrhage refers to discharging _____ in the _____.

8. Vascular is a term loosely meaning "vessel"—so cardio-vascular means _____ .
   cardio vascular

Check your responses with the answer key.

You now have twelve medical terms that can be linked with dozens of other terms to make hundreds of words. If someone tells you that:

You have psychosomatic symptoms of a cardio-vascular disease which the osteopath feels will not respond to hydrotherapy.

you will know that both psychological and physical elements (mind and body) are contributing to a disease of the vessels of the heart— and that one specialist says water-therapy or treatment can't touch that kind of difficulty.

42. You may be amused to see what can be done when many word elements are linked to form one word.

pneumnoultramicroscopicsilicovolcanoconiosis

You can break this apart into seven word elements.

pneumono ultra micro scopic silico volcano coniosis

and recognize probably all of these elements with the exception of **koniosis:** which means "dust." Actually, the word is generally written: pneumoconiosis and refers to a lung disease that comes from breathing mineral or metallic dusts over long periods of time.

43. *That* word you probably won't use too often! But many other words and phrases can be greatly clarified by examining the various word elements and getting a handle on their meanings. For example: In the 1940s biochemists labeled the chemical content of chromosomes: deoxyribonucleic acid or DNA—**deoxy-ribo-nucleic** acid.

You know that bio-chemists are chemists who study life and that chromosomes are the cell-centers responsible for carrying hereditary traits—but you may not be familiar with DNA. Along with its sister RNA, or ribonucleic acid, it is the fundamental material of life and the chemical basis of heredity and growth. The first one, DNA, merely adds the prefix **deoxy-** which means "less oxygen," to the rest of the word **ribonucleic. Ribose** is a kind of sugar and **nucleic** means "center."

So DNA and RNA are compounds of sugar-acids at the center of the cells, DNA having less oxygen than RNA, and RNA acting as a kind of messenger for DNA.

The whole, fantastic process of human growth and development can scarcely be traced in the limits of this little work, but the point is that understanding the terms can aid you tremendously if and when you *do* want to study the process. If so, you will be studying about such things as protein synthesis and ribosomes. You already have an understanding of the attitude and process that allows you to:

1. break the words into manageable elements
2. link the unknown to the known

Elements		Knowns
Protein	**pro-**	**pre:** "before" or "first"
	tein	**tain:** "to hold"
Synthesis	**syn-**	Greek prefix, same as **con-** meaning "with"
	thesis	"to put forth" as a theme
Ribosomes	**ribo-**	stated earlier, a kind of sugar
	some	in psychosomatic or chromosome—means "body"

Protein means literally "holding first place." Synthesis means "putting things together to form something new." Ribosomes are bodies active in the synthesis of protein; they are one of the **intra-cellular organelles** (within—cell—little-organs) or "little organs within the cells."

Remember, you can learn new material a great deal faster and retain it longer if you follow the guides of this book in learning what the words and phrases mean.

44. Making up Data Retention Cards for each word element will make it possible to link these elements more readily to new ones as they come along. For example, **ribo** and **some** should be on separate cards. Try rearranging the following word elements to form the complete words for both DNA and RNA.

oxy   de   acid   nuclei   ribo

DNA: _____   RNA: _____

45. Now that you have the technique of breaking words into elements, you will no longer be put off or frightened by such terms as:

    1. intravenous alimentation

    2. cancer viral etiology

    3. herpes simplex virus

    4. sickle cell anemia

    5. arteriosclerosis

You will recognize word elements that you already know. List the ones that look familiar from the above terms:

    1.

    2.

    3.

    4.

    5.

Check your list with the analysis below:

1. **Intra-** has been listed in this text. It means _____. **Venous** you can figure out by saying it aloud: it is the same as "vein," so intravenous means "within or inside the veins." You may be familiar with the "alimentary canal" which is the name of the digestive system from the mouth to the anus. This term, intravenous alimentation, refers to a method of providing adequate nourishment for persons through the veins rather than through the mouth.

2. You know that **logy** means_____ . Cancer is a term you are no doubt familiar with, but did you know that there are literally hundreds of different kinds of cancer! Some are very mild; some, of course, can be fatal. Exciting work is now being done with the viruses (viral) that possibly cause cancer. This is a study in etiology, or a study of one of the causes of cancer. Etiology, therefore, means "the study of causes."

3. One of the viral infections that is more bothersome than anything else is simply called *herpes simplex*—or more commonly, a "cold sore." It's not very serious.

4. Sickle cell anemia, on the other hand, can be very serious. Etiologists are working now to find out why some cells are lacking in

oxygen. These cells are actually shaped like sickles. Anemia

means _____.

5. Another poly-syllablic word—like alimentation (five syllables)—is arteriosclerosis (seven syllables)—but it, too, can be broken into understandable parts:

arterio	sclerosis
(as in arteries, tubes carrying blood away from the heart)	(to harden, same root as "skeleton")

You certainly will not have any difficulty handling such "little" words as:

coronary—pertaining to the heart

diabetes—literally "to go" (**betes**) "through" (**dia-**) the body. In diabetes, the sugar goes through the body very rapidly.

carcinomas—a malignant tumor—from the word for cancer

You will be able to distinguish very readily between:

benign—as in benefactor, benefit, benevolent—meaning "good"

malignant—as in malnutrition, malady—meaning "bad"

46. We are easily confused or frightened by things we do not understand. The words above make up a small portion of the medical terms you may run across in your lifetime, terms that refer to the state of health of you and your loved ones. You have the techniques now to make the unknown familiar to you—and therefore less frightening. That is one reason for familiarizing yourself with medical terms, whether you are going to specialize in the field or not.

47. If you are going to specialize in the health sciences, now is a good time to begin *and* continue building the basic vocabulary blocks of your profession. Listening, reading, asking questions and recording terms in your card system will speed your progress considerably!

48. Specialists in the field of medicine are like specialists in other fields: jazz, law, music, tennis. They use many terms in ways that are short-cuts for them. The words have specific meanings; knowing these meanings can help cut down on confusion, misunderstanding

and error. It is your duty to learn the special terms of the field in which you are interested. Using the best tools available, and the other guides of this book, you can break the barriers that can occur when you don't understand the vocabulary.

The Metric System

49. The time will probably come in the lives of all United States citizens when knowing the metric system will be essential. The metric system is a measurement system widely used throughout the world; it is simple and logical. The whole system is based on these six terms:

> **kilo** (1000)
> **hecto** (100)
> **deca** (10)
> **deci** (1/10)
> **centi** (1/100)
> **milli** (1/1000)
> **micro** (1/1,000,000)

50. The basic unit, the meter, is defined as:
    1. one ten-millionth of the distance from the north pole to the equator—a distance of about 6,200 miles
    2. about equal to thirty-nine and one-half of our inches.

    From the meter we get linear measurements or **meters**:

> **kilometer**—1000 meters
> **hectometer**—100 meters
> **decameter**—10 meters
> **decimeter**—.1 meter
> **centimeter**—.01 meter
> **millimeter**—.001 meter
> **micrometer**—.000001 meter

51. Another measurement is the measurement of volume or **liters**. One liter is defined as a cubic decimeter (1/10 of a meter).

52. The third measurement is of weight or **grams**. One gram is the weight of a cubic centimeter of water.

    A table can be set up as shown on page 190. Fill in the blanks.

	Meters (Linear Measurement)	Liters (Volume)	Grams (Weight)
kilo	kilometer	kiloliter	kilogram
hecto	hectometer	_____	_____
deca	_____	decaliter	_____
(one)	meter	liter	gram
deci	_____	_____	decigram
centi	centimeter	_____	_____
milli	_____	milliliter	_____
micro	(micron)	_____	microgram

53. Filling in the blanks is not difficult. And remembering what the metric system terms mean in words more common to us is not difficult for *some* of the terms. For example:

   (A) Since a cent is 1/100 of a dollar we won't have trouble remembering that **centi** means 1/100.

   (B) We use the word decade (ten years) so we won't have too much trouble remembering that **deca-** means ten.

   (C) We use **deci** in decimal—as a number *less* than one, a fraction or part of one, based on ten. So we won't have much trouble remembering that **deci** means 1/10.

   (D) We know **micro** means *very* small: **microscopic**, **microscope**, **micrometer** (pronounced mi**crom**eter).

   The last is a device for measuring *very* small amounts. **Micro** is not used as often in the metric system as the other terms, but it still can be useful to know that **micro** refers to very small measures— 1/1,000,000.

   Another one, **milli**, can be linked with our term million, which means "a thousand thousands." **Milli** means 1/1,000. It takes a thousand **milligrams** to make up one **gram**.

54. Four out of the five metric system terms we have dealt with so far signify measures *less* than one. What are they: (beginning initial is added to aid you)

D _____ 1/10

C _____ 1/100

M _____ 1/1000

M _____ 1/1,000,000

The fifth one **deca** means _____.

55. Now how about **kilo** and **hecto**? These do not have any very obvious referents in our measuring system. **Hecto** means hundred and **kilo** means thousand. The fact that **hecto** and **hundred** both start with *h* helps some. **Hecto** means "hundred." That leaves **kilo**. You will have to figure out your own mnemonic device. It is the largest one on the chart. **Kilo** means one thousand.

56. Now quickly fill in the meanings of each of the following terms in the metric system:

kilo means   _____

hecto means   _____

deca means   _____

deci means   _____

centi means   _____

milli means   _____

micro means   _____

Check your answers with the answer key on page 192.

57. Make up Data Retention Cards—and study them—on any you missed. When you are ready, take the following quiz.

1. A centimeter is a _____ of a meter.

2. Ten grams are written in the metric system as a _____

_____ .

3. One thousand meters are one _____ .

4. The smallest weight-measure on the chart is a _____-gram.

5. A deciliter is a _____ of a _____ .

Answer Key

56. **Kilo:** one thousand
Hecto: one hundred
Deca: ten
Deci: one-tenth
Centi: one-hundreth
Milli: one-thousandth
Micro: one-millionth

Answer Key

57. 1. hundreth
2. a decagram
3. kilometer
4. microgram
5. tenth, liter
6. liters
7. grams
8. meters
9. hectometer
10. milligram

6. Volume is measured in _____ .

7. Weight is measured in _____ .

8. Linear measurements are in _____ .

9. If you run 100 meters, you have run one _____ .

10. One one-thousandth of a gram of salt is called a _____ .

Check your responses with the answer key.

58. You may wish to make up Data Retention Cards on this section and file them away until the time when the United States converts to the metric system entirely. We are slowly making the conversion now. You will be ahead if you are familiar with the terms that much of the world now uses to make linear measurements, to measure weight, and to measure volume. The distance you travel from one town to another, the measure of the baking soda you put in a recipe, or the amount of water you add to your plant food may soon be stated in the metric system.

Foreign Words and Phrases

59. Throughout this book you have already run into a variety of words and phrases that could be called "foreign." Legal terms, such as:

> *de facto*—in fact
>
> *de jure*—by law
>
> *ad valorem*—according to the value

You will see and hear foreign words elsewhere, for example in reference to dining and drinking:

> *hors d'oeuvres* (pronounced **or**-dervs)—appetizers
>
> *entrée* (pronounced on-**tray**)—the main course

These are French and Latin, not English.

60. Some foreign terms you may see occasionally, but you may not want to use them yourself. They are pretentious, showy. Such terms as the following fall in this category:

> *in toto*—totally
>
> *en masse*—in a mass, in a group
>
> *ipso facto*—by the fact, or therefore
>
> *esprit de corps*—team spirit

61. Some foreign words *can* be used legitimately, as they are useful short-cuts to make specific things clear. Some of the foreign words in this category are:

   A. *Anno Domini (A.D.)* stands for in the year of our Lord (not "after death," as some people think. *If* they mean "after the death of Jesus," that would be about A.D. 33, which would be incorrect).

   B. *Avant-garde* means in the fore-guard. This may be a bit showy to us but you *do* see it in art and fashion books. It refers especially to styles that are ahead of their times.

   C. *Blitzkrieg* means a lightning war. This German term became used widely during the Second World War, referring to sudden and strong attacks by one side against another. You now may read about a "blitz" in football!

   D. *Déjà vu* (pronounced day-zah-voo) is the weird feeling that what is happening has happened before.

   E. *Idiot savant* (pronounced idiot-sah-vont) means a knowledge-able idiot. Cases have been recorded of persons who have very low IQs but who can do astounding things, such as add up all the numbers on boxcars as the train passes by.

   F. *Faux pas* (pronounced foe-pah) means a false step, a wrong move.

   G. *Gendarme* (pronounced zhan-darm)—this one may fall in the category of a term to be avoided; "policemen" will do as well. Gendarme is the French word for "policeman"; the gendarmerie is the police station.

   H. *In loco parentis* means in the place of parents. It refers especially to those duties which a college or university assumes as the "local parent." Soon there may be no need for the term.

   I. *Status quo* is the present state of things. Some politicians want to maintain the status quo; some want to go back one hundred years.

62. In one sense, ninety-nine percent of our words are "foreign words." We have very few words from the American Indian (tepee, wig-wam). But, of course, the ninety-nine percent have been largely absorbed so that they don't stand out as "foreign words." Avoid a word or phrase that still looks and sounds "foreign" if the same

thing can be said as concisely using a word or phrase that does not look or sound foreign.

63. Read over the preceding list of foreign words and phrases; when you are ready, try filling in the blanks on the following short quiz, using the eight words and phrases you have just studied.

1. My parents want to keep the _____.
   (present state of things)

2. If I go away to college, they expect the college to be my _____ (parent-

   _____.
   on-location)

3. When I have kids, I am not going to act like some _____ (French

   _____.
   policeman)

4. The new art show has some paintings that are very _____ (in the fore-

   _____.
   guard)

5. Some people don't know that A.D. is the abbreviation for the Latin words _____.
   (year of our Lord)

6. I really put my foot in my mouth; it was a terrible _____.
   (false step,
   wrong move)

7. The German term _____is now used more in football
   (lightning war)
   than in war games.

8. Some _____ can do amazing things, but they
   (idiots-knowledgeable)
   usually lose their skill by the time they become adults.

Check your responses with the answer key on page 196.

Answer Key

63. 1. status quo
2. in loco parentis
3. gendarme
4. avant-garde
5. anno domini
6. faux pas
7. blitzkreig
8. idiot savants

64. You may wish to look up in the dictionary those words you missed. Some foreign words are not listed: idiot savante, for example. You may have to go to a special dictionary of psychological terms to find it. Remember: avoid the unusual foreign word or phrase if a more customary word or phrase will do!

65. Make up new Data Retention Cards as new foreign words appear. In the next few years we may find that many words from the Orient (East) as well as the Occident (West) become important for us to know!

Chapter 9

Experiment with Words—

Enjoy Learning

1. In the last chapter words were offered to you in categories: business and legal words, medical terms, and so on. But generally that is not the way words appear to you. They come more often in a hodge-podge. You hear a new word in conversation or read a new word in a newspaper. You see advertisements and hear sales pitches. You are bombarded by words.

2. If you can experiment with the words that are new to you, if you can use the Learning Techniques in this text, you will find that these new words can become *your* words. You will have fun doing it because you now have special skills. You now have the tools to recognize common roots and affixes in many new words. You can enjoy using your ability to break words apart and practice those parts you don't know. You now can use Data Retention Cards to keep in your mind the word elements you want to remember.

3. You know to use as many senses as you can: to visualize words, to say them aloud, to write them down. That is how *unknown* words become *known* words.

4. To experiment with words is a continual process. And it is one that can go on almost any place: in front of the television, in the car, in a lecture hall, in a conversation.

5. For example, if someone suggests to you that you are gaining a great deal of expertise in vocabulary building, do you nod and then begin experimenting with the word expertise? Do you consider, for example, that expertise has the words **pert** and **expert** in it?

6. Or if someone mentions the numerous atrocities of war, does it occur to you that there is a **city** in atro**city**.

7. If you read a sign:

PRESTIGE LOCATION
IMMEDIATE OCCUPANCY

199

as you drive along a downtown street, do you break the words apart and play around with these parts:

1. Immediate: What does "media" have to do with immediate?
2. How many other forms does occupancy have: occupy, occupant, occupational therapy, occupation, re-occupy . . .
3. Is the **pre-** in prestige the same as the **pre-** in **pre**-warning?
4. What other terms have the same root as location: locale, localize, local option, local anesthetic . . .

Even though you may not be able to get immediate feedback on your questions, you still will be taking advantage of your skill in linking various knowns into the formation of new words—or new understandings of old words.

8. What does **pert** have to do with expertise? Or what do **cities** have to do with atrocities? What does "before" or **pre-** have to do with prestige? Well, as a matter of fact, not much.

9. But the point is that experimenting with words can aid you in spelling, in linking roots to other words, in shifting affixes around, and in increasing your word power.

10. Take the word atrocity. Besides **city**, what else can you do in breaking apart or adding to the word? Do you know the word

   atrocious

   as in "That's **atrocious** behavior" (pronounced ah-**tro**-shus, meaning "awful, nasty"). By changing the suffix _____ to _____ you have changed a noun into an adjective:

   atrocity (noun) to atrocious (adjective)

11. And expertise (pronounced: ex-per-tease)? You can recognize the word expert in it; the expert has a lot of expertise, or special knowledge, as in "She has a lot of expertise in accounting procedures."

12. Now go back to some of the first Learning Techniques in this book:

   Chapter 2: Break words into syllables; say them aloud:

   ex-per-tise (pronounced: ex-per-tease)

   a-tro-cious (pronounced: ah-tro-shus)

   Examine words in context; figure out their meaning:

   "She has a lot of expertise in accounting procedures."

   "That is atrocious behavior."

Chapter 3: Look for knowns within a word so you can use what you already know to apply to new situations:

expertise   and   **atroc**ity
                                    atrocious

Five Learning Techniques followed the ones listed above. Starting with Chapter 4, list as many as you can below. (**Hint:** What are the DRC cards designed to help you do?)

   1. Chapter 4:

   2. Chapter 5:

   3. Chapter 6:

   4. Chapter 7:

   5. Chapter 8:

13. Check your memory with the chapter headings on the Contents page at the beginning of the book. (Fill in any Learning Techniques you had forgotten.) Then place a check mark on the columns to the right under:

   1. if you remember the technique

   2. if you find that learning technique helpful

Chapter Number	Learning Technique	Remembered	Find Helpful
4			
5			
6			
7			
8			

14. The ones you find helpful—and hopefully they will all help—you will want to keep in mind as you experiment with words, now and for the rest of your life! You know that these Learning Techniques apply to all kinds of learning besides learning vocabulary. But just applying them to the retention of vocabulary terms *alone* will assist you in understanding yourself and the words around you.

15. You may be a bit confused by this last Learning Technique: *Experiment with Words: Enjoy Learning.* You have so far in this chapter

six samples of the kinds of words you can experiment with—words that could at any time appear on your auditory or visual receptacles (that is, you could hear or see them).

Word	Syllables	Meaning
expertise	3	skill, knowledge
atrocious	3	awful, inhuman
atrocity	4	violence, brutality
prestige	2	elite, well thought of
location	3	site, place
immediate	4	now
occupancy	4	live within

The more *word-conscious* you become, the more you experiment with these and other words, the more you will increase your ability to use words.

16. These may seem like a strange assortment of terms. But that's how words appear as we work and study and play. They come from all over the place. We will not always be presented with neat lists of terms that apply in one certain field. We will meet words in all sorts of places. And the better we are at doing these things:

    1. breaking them apart

    2. finding the parts we know

    3. linking them to other word elements—as we have done on the word wheels

    4. finding out whether or not we are on the right track

    5. practicing the new or unknown parts

the more we feel a justifiable reward for our increasing expertise in word usage.

17. Remember especially—and incorporate into your learning style—the power of your own good head and all your senses. Remember to say words aloud, hear them, get the feel of them on your tongue. Move them around in your mind's eye, visualize their meanings. Even in the quiet of a final examination in college, or in a placement test for a job, whispering a word to yourself may help you psyche out the meaning.

18. A student missed an exam question completely because he was not capable of sounding out, of recognizing that the word had the same root as another word he knew very well. The word on the exam was

agrarian

Had he experimented with the word, had he sounded it out, he said that he would have recognized the word as having the same root as:

agriculture

The question concerned the Agrarian Revolt. He didn't think the word through, he failed to sound it out, so he didn't figure out that the Agrarian Revolt had to do with the Farmer's Revolt, which he knew about. **Ag**rarian, **ag**riculture. So he got zero points for that question. Too bad.

19. Stop for a minute. How do you:

(1) *Incorporate* things into your learning style?

(2) *Psyche out* the meaning of something?

20. The word incorporate you probably already know. How many words can you link with it? **In-**, the prefix, you know, means either

_____ or _____. How about the root word **corp** that you had in Chapters 7 and 8, (habeas corpus)? What words or phrases can you link it with: (keeping in mind that **corp** means "body")?

        corporation
        unincorporated
        Marine Corps
        esprit de corps (pronounced es-pree duh-core)
        Corpus Christi
        corps de ballet (core-duh-bahl-lay)

Can you add others?

_____

_____

_____

_____

How about corpse? A body, indeed—a dead body. How about corporal? (May have meant "leader of a body of troops.") Do you

Answer Key
23. 1. agriculture or farming
2. knowledge, experience
3. awful, inhuman brutalities
4. corps: corporation, unincorporated, Marine Corps, corps de ballet
5. figure them out

know the word corpulence meaning a "fat body?" How about corpuscle, a very small body or cell.

21. The slang use of psych, as in "psyche out," has come into the language only recently. In Chapter 2 you learned that the word psychology had two roots, **psych** and **logy**. To psyche out the instructor simply means to figure out his methods.

22. These last terms agrarian, incorporate, and psych out appeared in this chapter. By experimenting with these three terms, you can put together fifteen or twenty words and phrases just as a starter. Experimentation with words is not only fun, but provides rich learning also.

23. So far you have a hodge-podge of words taken from conversations, from signboards, from exam questions, from this text. Now try the following quiz from the words from these various areas:

1. Agrarian has to do with _____ .

2. To have a lot of expertise is to have a lot of _____

   _____ .

3. Atrocious behavior is _____ behavior; atrocities are _____ .

4. The Latin word for "body" is _____ and appears in such English words as: _____

   _____ .

5. To psyche out the meanings of words means to _____

   _____ .

Try linking the following words with the meanings on the right that you think are most appropriate. Check answers on page 206.

1. psychosomatic   _____ over-weight

2. corpulence   _____ farmers warring against restrictions

3. atrocities   _____ having to do with mind and body

4. Agrarian revolt   _____ minute particles, small bodies

5. corpuscle   _____ inhuman, cruel acts

Answer Key
24. 4.
3.
2.
5.
1.
6.

None of these are very closely related; it would be hard to write a sensible paragraph incorporating all five terms. But any one of these terms can be juggled about, experimented with. And from such experimenting, knowledge grows.

24. Now try this one. Someone says: "He is certainly vociferous." What little words—or roots—do you recognize in **vociferous** (pronounced vo-sif-er-us)? You know the word **vocal** and you have studied the

root **fer** in this text. **Fer** means_____. So you can figure out that vociferous means "carrying the voice." The vociferous person talks a great deal.

How many words can you make by adding various prefixes and suffixes to:

Vociferous

voc	fer
_____	_____
_____	_____
_____	_____
_____	coniferous (cone-bearing, a kind of tree, like pine trees)

Remember that the mnemonic device for **fer** was "ferry" boat—something that *bears* you across. To "refer" to something is to *carry* it back; a referendum is the process of *carrying* a proposed law *back* to the people to vote on. Check the words you wrote down using **voc** and **fer** with the list below:

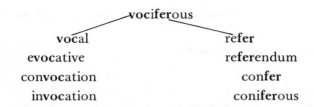

vo**c**al   re**fer**

evocative   referendum

convocation   confer

invocation   coniferous

You can also change the *c* to a *k* in **voc** and get:

invoke—to call *in* a higher power

revoke—to call something *back*

and you can change the prefixes on the **fer** words and get:

> conference
> reference
> deference

Knowing the meanings of prefixes as you do (check your DRCs at this point if necessary), try the following matching quiz. Check answers on page N-206.

1. evocative (prefix: **ex-**)	_____ to call something back
2. conference	_____ a calling together
3. convocation	_____ hearing with, carrying things together (ideas, plans . . .)
4. revoke	_____ carrying down or away; also submitting to another
5. deferent	_____ bringing out or calling forth memories
6. vociferous	_____ carrying a lot of voice, noisy, verbose, talkative

In the second column above, last line, the word: **verbose.** Did you examine it in context; did you notice the synonym "talkative" after it? Did you try to think of other words using the root: **verb?**

25. Earlier, **verbum** meant "word." Now it refers to just certain words, but we use the root **verb** in:

> **verb**atim—word-for-word, an exact recording of what someone said

> **verb**iage—ad**verb**—pro**verb**

26. Or a more complicated example: Let's say someone asks you if you think that Henry Ford was truly philanthropist. What are you going to answer? If you remember from Chapter 5 that **anthropo** is the Greek word for "man," that **phil** means "a kind of love."

> phil (love) anthrop (man) ist (one who)

A philanthropist is one who loves mankind (today it means specific-ally one who shows his love by giving lots of money away)!

27. Now you are ready to experiment with the word philanthropist.

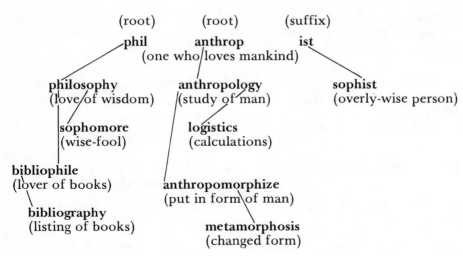

28. You can now check your knowledge of the various roots and affixes, looking up the ones that you do not know, practicing them, making them all a fixed part of your word knowledge.

29. These are merely samples of the kinds of words that may appear in conversations and readings. You will have to add to the list on your own—from now on! *You* are the one who will make the experimenting useful to you. Try the following quiz to see how you are doing so far.

30. From the list on the right, select the appropriate meaning for the **roots** in **bold** in the list on the left; write that meaning in the blank following the word list:

Word List	Meaning of Root	List of Possible Meanings
1. **loca**tion	_____	carrying
2. **corpor**ation	_____	middle
3. **psych**ologist	_____	mind, behavior
4. **voci**ferous	_____	calling, voice
5. phil**anthrop**ist	_____	wise
6. **verb**ose	_____	word
7. **soph**omore	_____	body
8. **med**ian	_____	place, site
9. **refer**endum	_____	friend or lover

31. Fill in the blanks below using the following words: location, corporation, psychologist, vociferous, philanthropist, verbose, sophomore, median, and referendum.

    1. The _____ asked his friend, the _____ to
          (lover of man)   (expert in behavior)

      suggest a _____ for a _____ that could
                 (site)   (body, institution)

      benefit freshmen and _____ with _____ skills.
                          (wise fools)   (average, middle)

    2. If you took a _____, you might find that many
                 (vote)

      people think of _____ as meaning *over*-wordy,
                 (word)

      whereas _____ means expressing strong opinions.
        (calling, voice)

32. Now try some on your own:

    1. You read that the gestation (pronounced jes-tay-shun) period of the female elephant is twenty-two months, that of the human female about nine months. You can figure out that the gestation period is the period of_____ —or the period of time for carrying the young in the womb. What other words use the root **gest** meaning "bearing" or "carrying."

      (**gest**)

    2. Try the word obdurate meaning "hardened." It generally refers to attitudes rather than things. You read: "The judge's attitude was obdurate," and you wonder what it means? You remember the prefix **ob-** in Chapter 5, meaning "against" (among other things). **Dur**, as the root, isn't very **hard** to figure out; put them together and you have "hardened against." Now make some other words using both the prefix **ob-** and the root **dur**.

                  obdurate

      _____   _____

    _____   _____

Now check your word wheels—or inverted pyramids—with the ones below.

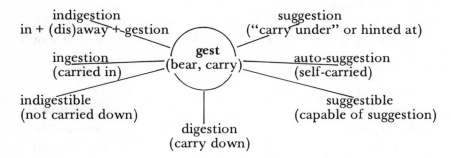

indigestion
in + (dis)away +-gestion

suggestion
("carry under" or hinted at)

gest
(bear, carry)

ingestion
(carried in)

auto-suggestion
(self-carried)

indigestible
(not carried down)

suggestible
(capable of suggestion)

digestion
(carry down)

Even gesticulate—as in "he gesticulated wildly" meaning "gestured," or "waved his hands around"—comes from the same root.

2. **Obdurate** (hardened, pronounced ob-dur-ut)

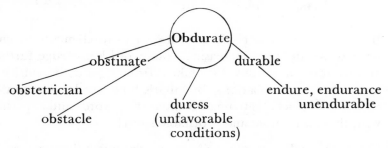

Obdurate

obstinate

durable

obstetrician

endure, endurance
unendurable

obstacle

duress
(unfavorable
conditions)

Note that **ob-** links with the root **sta** or **ste**, meaning "to stand," forming the word obstetrician (ob-stu-**tri**-shun) or obstetrics. The **ob**stetrician delivers babies (formerly the mid-wife); the term comes from "standing before."

33. So far in this chapter you have experimented with two general groups of words:

1. Words you already know and can make other words from:

Group 1	Other words from same root
location	locale, locate, local
immediate	media, mediate, immediately
occupation	occupy, occupational therapy
incorporate	corpse, corporation
psyche out	psychology

2. Words that may not have been as familiar to you but that have some word elements you can recognize or some similar words that you know:

Group 2	Prefix	Root	Similar Words
atrocity	a-		atrocious
expertise	ex-		expert
agrarian			agriculture
vociferous		voc	vocal, voice
verbatim			verb (word)
philanthropist		phil (love of)	philosophy
		anthropo (man)	
gestation			digestion
obdurate	ob-		durable
obstetrician	ob-	ste	stand

In both groups you could link known word elements to unknown or new words, thus increasing your word knowledge further. The groups form a motley list—taken from signboards, office doors, newspapers, conversations. But that's how words come to us—from all over the place. Watching for interesting words and experimenting with them is a varied and profitable sport!

34. Words that fall in the first group, words already known, can be very beneficial to experiment with, breaking the word apart and linking prefixes and other word elements to it. For example, you are familiar with the word suicide. Do you also know the word genocide? Well, you know the word **gene**; you studied it at the beginning of Chapter 8. Knowing that

suicide means "killing oneself"

and that **gene** comes from the root meaning "race" or "kind," you

can probably figure out that genocide means _____

_____. So **cide** must refer to "murder of" or "killing."

Then when you see words like

> regicide (**regis**: king)
> matricide (**matri**: mother)
> patricide (**patri**: father)

you will know that someone is getting murdered. You can reinforce that learning the next time you pick up a spray can to kill insects,

called an _____.

Place the six **cide** words on a word wheel:

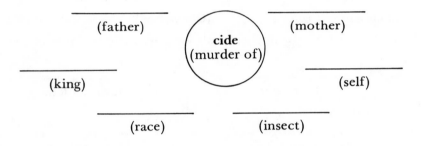

35. Also beneficial is experimenting with words that fall in the second group above, words that may not be familiar to you but may contain some word elements that you recognize. Let's say that you see the word: hierarchy. If you sound it out, you will get at once the "higher" sound at the beginning. And it fits: **hier** means "sacred" but now generally refers to ranking things from high to low, or low to high. For example: "The army has a hierarchy from a private to a five-star General." **Arch**, you know, is a "form used in construction," usually "to span something." So a hierarchy is:

hier	**archy**	a form for listing things from
(from higher to lower)	(form)	high to low—or low to high

You have a hierarchy of things in your own life; sometimes you call it "listing priorities."

The prior things (first things) come ahead of the others. You spend your time on the things that are high up on your hierarchy.

36. Knowing hierarchy, you see a couple of days later the word matriarchy. **Arch** you recognize again. **Matri** you just learned means

_____ . So is matriarchy a "form of mothers?" No, because **arch** has another meaning. It also means "chief," "ruler," or "beginning." So a matriarchy is a society that is _____

_____ . How about a patriarchy? Who rules

in a patriarchy? _____ Do you remember the prefix **ana-** meaning "outside of" or "without?" Would you expect an anarchist

form of government to have lots of rules _____ or to be pretty

much without rules _____ ? (Check one)

37. Now make up a word wheel with your **arch** words:

(father ruled)   **arch**   (mother ruled)
                    (chief, ruler)

(without rules)   (one ruled)

Another **arch** meaning "beginning" is **archeo**. So the study of man's

beginnings is called _____ .
                        (beginning—study of)

38. **Arch** means two things: _____

and _____ . List below the words from the previous paragraph that use each meaning.

Arch meaning a form, to span something	Arch meaning chief, ruler or beginning
_____	_____
_____	_____
_____	_____
_____	_____
_____	_____

Then add any other words you know that you think use one of these two forms of **arch**. You may not be able to fill up all the slots, but you should be able to add some words from your own word knowledge.

Arcade—"a series of arches forming a walk-way."

Archaic—"ancient, from the beginning or no longer in use."

Which column does each of these belong in? Of course, arcade in column one and archaic in column two.

39. Check your dictionary for any other words you may have listed and are not sure about. By experimenting with just these two words, the known word suicide and the possibly unknown word hierarchy, you have made almost two dozen words, depending on how many you added to the columns above.

40. Let's assume that you are sufficiently familiar with the words in the first group: location, immediate, occupation, incorporate, psyche out, suicide. If you need further help on any of them, make up Data Retention Cards and check your dictionary to be sure you are on the right track.

41. The ten words in Group 2 may need a bit more practice. So try filling in the blanks in the following sentence with words from the list of ten given below. You will note that the words have been grouped in six nouns and four adjectives, and that the blanks are labeled noun or adjective. So choose a word from either the noun list or the adjective list and write it in the blank provided.

Noun List	Adjective List
atrocity	agrarian
expertise	vociferous
philanthropist	verbatim
gestation	obdurate
obstetrician	

The only changes you can make are changing singular nouns to plural ones, as atrocity to atrocities.

1. The _____ said that the period of _____
           noun   noun

_____was entirely too long.

2. The _____ Revolt was labeled by those
   adjective

   _____ as characterized by _____
   noun   adjective

   _____ farmers calling loudly for specific reforms.

3. The _____ gave a _____
   noun   adjective

   account of the _____ .
   noun

4. His_____attitude made him disliked by
   adjective

   all.

Did you figure out that in experimenting with this word list, you
had choices for all the blanks except those in number 2? Once you
read that the *farmers* were *calling loudly,* you almost had to use the
terms agrarian and vociferous. So that sentence reads:

> The **Agrarian** Revolt was labeled by those with **expertise** as
> characterized by **vociferous** farmers calling loudly for specific
> reforms.

But in experimenting with the others you had some choices:

> 1. The **obstetrician** said that the period of **gestation** was entire-
>   ly too long.
>   or:
> 1. The **philanthropist** said that the period of **atrocities** was
>   entirely too long.

Only the philanthropist or the obstetrician could "say it" because
only they are people; the other nouns refer to events, skills, periods.

> 3. The philanthropist gave a **verbatim** account of the **atrocity.**
>   or:
> 3. The obstetrician gave a **vociferous** account of the **philan-
>   thropist.**

Any of the adjectives *could* work on number 4, but a "verbatim
attitude" doesn't make much sense. "Vociferous" or "obdurate"
would fit best.

42. Sometimes experimenting with words such as these can get ridiculous. But it can also be fun. And the learning still takes place. *That,* after all, is what we are after.

43. You may want to check some of the other words in your dictionary, jotting down notes on these pages or at the back of the book as you go along. You may wish to make up new Data Retention Cards for new roots you run into as you experiment with words. But you should check your dictionary for accuracy when you experiment with new words.

44. For example, you may see the word amalgamated, as in Amalgamated Steel Workers Union of America. So you begin investigating the word amalgamated. You first of all:

    1. break the word into syllables:

    a-mal-gam-a-ted

    and then you:

    2. examine the word in context to see if you can figure out what it means.

    Then you:

    3. look for some knowns within the word and you may come up with:

    a—away from, outside of

    mal—bad

    gam—could it be the same as the **gam**
    in bi**gam**y, mono**gam**y

    so you try putting it together: "away from a bad marriage"—amalgamated.

    Amalgamated does mean "together" or "consolidated, combined." But the root is **amalgama** meaning "mixture." In this case the experimenting with the word didn't exactly fit the data given in the dictionary. But it did provide a good mnemonic device for remembering that amalgamated means something like "togetherness."

45. Another way to experiment with words to build word power and understanding is to try putting many-syllable words in place of one syllable words or vice versa. Often the multi-syllabic word will have Latin and Greek affixes, which you now know. For example, a sign in the joke shops reads:

    Eschew Obfuscation

which means: "put down confusion" or "keep things simple." Or you could have a sign:

**Maintain Americophillic Attitudes or Deportation
Will Be Rendered Essential!**

which can be simplified to:

American—Love It or Leave It!

**Engender Amatory Presentations
in Preference to Bellicose Operations**

which simply means

Make Love Not War.

From the above you have the following words with prefixes and roots:

Prefixes	Roots
obfuscation (against)	main**tain** (ten) (hold)
deportation (down, away)	**phillic** (love of)
engender (same as in-)	de**port**ation (carry)
presentations (before)	en**gender**ed (generate)
preference (before)	**amat**ory (love)
	pre**ference** (bear, carry)
	bellicose (war)

46. And still another way to explore words is to make up abbreviations or acronyms.

You remember the terms:

Synonyms: words that mean approximately the same
Antonyms: words that mean approximately the opposite
Homonyms: words that sound the same

But what is an **acronym**? You recognize the same root: **nym**; so what about **acro-**? Well, **acro-** means "height" or "summit." In this sense, it refers to the beginning letter of each word within a group, as in:

SCUBA—*S*elf-*C*ontained *U*nderwater *B*reathing *A*pparatus

Governmental agencies abound with acronyms. For example, within the United States Government we have:

ZIP—Zone Improvement Program—for speeding the mail

HUD—Housing and Urban Development

just to name two. These differ from abbreviations that do *not* make a word but stand simply as individual letters:

F.B.I.—Federal Bureau of Investigation

F.D.I.C.—Federal Deposit Insurance Corporation

The acronyms are more fun. Sometimes they have curious meanings:

COP—*C*areer *O*pportunities *P*rogram

and sometimes they are designed to change assumed meanings:

PIG—*P*ride, *I*ntegrity, and *G*uts

Sometimes they have meanings that are known far outside the boundaries of the United States.

NATO—North Atlantic Treaty Organization

SEATO—South-East Asia Treaty Organization

UNESCO—United Nations Educational, Scientific and Cultural Organization

47. Sometimes the meanings are so specific or scientific that even when we know what the letters stand for, we still may not understand the terms. For example,

LASER—*L*ight *A*mplification by *S*timulated *E*mission of *R*adiation

RADAR—*R*adio *D*etecting *a*nd *R*anging

In the field of data processing, a kind of elongated acronym crops up; knowing the full name does not always help us understand the meaning of the term. For example, FORTRAN means "formula translation," COBOL means "common business oriented language." We still would have to know quite a bit more about the nature of computer language before these acronyms would mean much to us.

48. But acronyms can be fun to both unlock and create. By unlocking the meaning of some acronyms, you can get a better understanding of the subject at hand.

49. You can create "words" from all sorts of sources. For instance, take the last four chapters of this text:

R—Reward yourself

U—Use the best tools available

S—Study the things you are interested in learning

P—Play around with words.

The first letter of each Learning Technique makes R.U.S.P.—or RUSP. Sometimes the kind of nonsense acronyms make can help you recall information.

50. So unlocking the acronyms that others have formed can be challenging and helpful. And creating your own acronyms can be not only fun but also useful in studying.

51. You have a variety of ways to experiment with words.

   (A) Words you already know and with which you can make other words.

   (B) Words you are not sure about but in which you can recognize some elements.

   (C) Big words that you can make into small words—and vice versa.

   (D) Acronyms that can either unlock or be created on your own. These kinds of words come from a variety of sources. They are a miscellany.

52. Maybe you love to read history books; in so doing, you run into words like **medieval** and **renaissance** in modern, western civilization or **neolithic** and **paleolithic** in ancient times. Breaking the words apart, recognizing known elements, and linking the unknown to them, can speed your grasp on many historical terms. For example, to these terms: medieval, renaissance, neolithic, paleolithic, you can apply the learning principles from this text.

53. Renaissance has the prefix _____ meaning _____ . Does **naissance** look like anything you've seen before? Change the **nai** to **nat** and what can you come up with.

   Words using root **nat**:   _____

   _____

   _____

How about **natural**? You have also seen these terms in this text:

   innate: born into

   natal: birth

   pre-natal care: care before birth

So you can probably figure out that **nat** is from the root meaning "born" or "natural." **Naissance** is a form of **nat. Re-:** "back," "again;" **naissance:** "born."

The Renaissance period, roughly from 1400 to 1650, was not exactly a "re-birth," as the prefix and root state. For a "re-birth" suggests that there was a death. The period just before the Renaissance was full of all sorts of goodies: Chaucer the poet, in England; Giotto the painter, in Italy; Thomas Aquinas the philosopher, in Italy; to name but three. It was not a "dead" time. Some may consider these and their contemporaries as Renaissance men, but the point is that a clear-cut Renaissance beginning does not exist.

54. But the Renaissance was a kind of re-flowering or spreading of culture. Increased trade, more stable cultural centers supporting the arts, the development of printing presses were some of the devices that made this spread of culture possible. So we came to call this period from around 1450 to 1650 the "Renaissance."

55. So with the term "Medieval." You can recognize the word element **media** in the term, although the *a* has changed to *e*. **Media** means "middle." This refers to the period roughly preceding the Renaissance period. But again, it is really not the "middle" of anything. It's hard to imagine a "middle" to the two-million-or-so years of human history that we know about so far. So the term medieval must be taken lightly. It generally refers to the period in western civilization from the fifth century to about the fifteenth century— or 400 to 1400 A.D.

56. Your history books can fill you in on the fascinating flow of people and events during these times. But having some word-attacks that you can use on terms from history will help you remember what you study.

57. Remember in Chapter 3 that prehistoric means "before *recorded* history?" From the study of prehistoric people, some loosely defined periods are described: paleolithic—"old stone age," neolithic—"new stone age."

So **paleo** means _____ and **neo** means _____ .

Lith, you can figure out from the above, means _____ .
Each of these two periods has characteristics that set it apart from another period. For example, the people who lived in the Old

Stone Age or _____ period used stone tools

that had been chipped on the edges to make them more efficient.

And the people who lived in the New Stone Age or _____

_____ period used more advanced stone instruments, such as stones with wood handles, and also knew something about farming. They were not as dependent on berry-gathering and hunting as were their ancestors. Just as we do not have to go out and pump the water and chop the wood as did many of our ancestors only 100 years ago.

58. More time separates the Paleolithic people from the Neolithic people than separates us from the Old Testament figures of Moses and Abraham. And from what we know today, both periods went on for, at least, several thousand years. When we use words like Paleolithic, Neolithic, as well as medieval and renaissance, we need to be cautious. The terms are not rigid labels. We would be amused to know that future histories labeled our times as:

> 1750-1944: Industrial Revolution
>
> 1944-1968: Atomic Revolution
>
> 1969-2000: Space Revolution

as if a clear age dawned on one particular day or within one special year. It just doesn't happen that way. But knowing and being able to apply common historical terms can help you place events on a time-line, putting them in relation one to another, and thus keeping them more firmly in your mind for future reference.

59. Some who are interested in the study of how we arrived at our present stage—that is, in studying history—are put off by some of the poorly identified terms that are used to refer to various people in the past. Some terms are easy: the Greeks, the Romans, and the Egyptians can still be identified on a map. But many labels for groups of people no longer appear on modern maps. So we get confused, or mystified (as in "mystery"). Not understanding what the terms refer to, we have trouble figuring out who fits where. If we try to fit groups of people into certain periods, we can start with these rough categories:

> Ancient: up to 500 A.D. (2 million B.C. to 500 A.D.)
>
> Medieval: 500 up to 1500 A.D.
>
> Modern: 1500 A.D. to present and . . . future. (includes the Renaissance period)

60. Some of the labels are confusing if not learned carefully. You may wish to consult your dictionary—or your history text—for further detail.

Labels for Groups of People	Period:	Who Lived in What Is Now
Celts (Celtic)	Ancient	Europe, British Isles
Druids	Ancient	France and England (perhaps mythical)
Franks	Medieval	Germany and France
Gaels (Gaellic)	Ancient	Scotland and Ireland
Gauls	Ancient	France and Belgium
Huns	Medieval	Asians who invaded Europe—setting in motion the Barbarian migrations
Normans	Medieval	Scandinavia (Norway, Denmark, Sweden); later France and Italy
Norseman	Ancient to Medieval	Scandinavia
Prussians	Modern	Germany (northern)
Rus	Medieval	Northmen—or Norse (they first unified Russia.)
Teutons	Ancient to Modern	Europe (northern)
Vikings	Medieval	Scandinavia
Welsh	Ancient to Modern	Western England (Wales)

61. Because of the strengths of these folk, as well as of the Africans and the Angles, the Indians and the Spanish, the Saxons and the Danes— as well as many others—we have the language we speak today.

62. You are further reminded by the chart above that history—and language—are not static things. People move: the Huns out of Asia, the Normans out of Scandinavia, the Rus across Russia. As people move, so does their language. It moves and changes and adapts to new times.

63. So with us. We will move deeper into and farther out from our globe, not to mention our fantastic transciency around the globe. We will add thousands of new words from many sources. You now have one of the most valuable techniques for creating and understanding these new words—a knowledge of the most frequently used word elements from our scientific and literary heritage.

64. Whether you are a student or a worker or a voter or a priest—or all of these—you will be able to deal more effectively with the world around you if you understand the vocabulary that world deals with. So continue to experiment with words, to enjoy learning new words, and to add them to your card and memory files.

65. We would not go so far as to say:

    Get the words and the rest will take care of itself.

    But we could say:

    Get the words and the rest will come a lot easier!

66. There is no chapter quiz over all of Chapter 9. There is a tear-out quiz in the back of the book.

    Among other things, you need to know the following roots:

gam	marriage	**gest**	give birth
gene	heredity	**arch**	ruler, beginning
cide	murder	**matri**	mother
phil	brotherly love	**nat, nasci**	born

    When you are ready to take it, do so. You might even want to make up some quizzes on your own, working especially in those fields that interest you.

67. Continue applying the Learning Techniques you have learned in this book, and you will continue to enjoy the rich rewards of expanding word power!

Master List: Prefixes

Prefix	Simple Meaning	Sample Word	Page
a-	outside of	amoral	63
ab-	away, away from	abstain	51
ad-	to, toward	advance	57, 83
anti-	against	anti-war	155
auto-	self	automobile	33
bi-	two	bicycle	29
circum-	around	circumference	49
com-	with	commission	105
de-	down, away	depress	53
dis-	apart, not	disquiet	53
ex-	formerly, out of	ex-spouse	3, 83
extra-	out of	extramarital	161
eu-	good	eulogy	120
hetero-	different	heterosexual	107
homo-	same	homogenized	107
hyper-	above, very	hyperactive	101
hypo-	under, below	hypodermic	101
in-	into, within	inborn	87
in-	not	invisible	87
inner-	within	inner-city	101
intra-	within	intramural	101
inter-	between	interracial	101
iso-	equal, similar	isometrics	147
mono-	one	monogamy	29
o-, ob-	against, away from	obliterate	122
non-	not	non-accredited	33
per-	thoroughly	perversion	103
poly-	many	polygamy	29
pre-	before	prescribe	23
pro-	before, in favor of	procession	103
re-, retro-	back, again	rejuvenate	23
sub-	under, below	subnormal	33, 83
trans-	across	transfer	33
un-	not	unnatural	87

Master List: Roots

English Root	Classical Root (GK: Greek L: Latin)	Simple Meaning	Sample Word	Page
anthropo	GK: anthropos	man	anthropology	208
arch	GK: arkhein	ruler, beginning	archeology	214
astro	GK: astron	star	astrology	99
bio	GK: bios	life	biology	89
cap	L: capere	to take or seize	capture	54
cide	L: caedere	to kill	suicide	212
corps	L: corpus	body	corpse	161
cosmos	GK: cosmo	universe, world	cosmonaut	99
derm	GK: derma	skin	hypodermic	111
dic, dict	L: dicere	to speak; word	diction	5
duc	L: ducere	to lead	conduct	23,113
fer	L: ferre	to bear or carry	transfer	113
gam	GK: gamos	marriage	bigamist	61,113
gene	GK: genos	smallest unit of heredity	generation	168
gest	L: gerere	to bear	gestation	210
gnos	L: gnoscere	to know	cognition	67
graph	GK: graphein	to write	graphology	99
ject	L: jacere	to throw	injection	55
log	GK: legein	to study, the science of	biology	29
media	L: medius	middle	medial strip	147
metrics	GK: metron	to measure	metric system	147
miss, mitt	L: mittere	to send	missionary	47
mon	L: monere	to warn	premonition	52
mort	L: mors	death	mortality	175
nasci	L: natus, nasci	to be born	Renaissance	61
neuro	L: neur	nerves	neurologist	61
nym	L: nomen	name	synonym	155
path	GK: pathos	sickness, feeling	sympathy	155
pli, plic	L: plicare	to fold	pliable	57
pon, pos	L: ponere	to put or place	component	57
port	L: portare	to carry	portable	57
press	L: pressare	to push	depression	39
psych	GK: psyche	mind, behavior	psychology	61

English Root	Classical Root	Simple Meaning	Sample Word	Page
rog	L: rogare	to ask	interrogate	135
scrib	L: scribere	to write	scribble	48
socio	L: socium	society	socialize	97
spect	L: specere	to look	spectacles	48
sta, sti	L: statuere	to stand	statue	128
ten	L: tenere	to have or hold	retention	67
theo	GK: theos	god, gods	theology	65, 97
vers, vert	L: vertere	to turn	subvert	45
verb	L: verbum	word	verbal	208
voc	L: vocare	to call	vocal	5

Master List: Suffixes

Word	Simple Meaning	Sample Word	Page
-able, ible	capable of, able to	trainable	137,139
-al	process, act of doing	revival	137,139
-ance, ence	condition, quality of	credence	137
-ant	one who believes or acts	applicant	137
-ate	to act or possess	create	137
-ful	have in abundance	plentiful	137
-ism	doctrine or belief in	socialism	136,137
-ist	one who believes	socialist	136,139
-itis	inflammation of	appendicitis	137
-ize	to make similar to	lionize	137
-ness	quality or condition	tiredness	137
-ous	possessing, full of	contemptuous	137
-ship	status or function	friendship	137
-tion	act or process	deception	137
-wise	position, or connection with	time-wise	137

Master Quiz: Chapter 1

Fill in the blanks in the following sentences with the most appropriate terms and the number of each term from the list below. See example number 1.

1. An (8) <u>introvert</u> does not talk about his feelings; an ( ) _____

    _____ will discuss his feelings freely.

2. If a person has deep and constant fears that people are plotting

    against him, he may be said to be ( ) _____ .

3. Any of us may have ( ) _____ tendencies at

    some time in our lives; on the other hand, _____ tendencies are far more serious and may require professional help.

4. If a certain behavior disgusts you, if it "turns you off," you could

    call that behavior ( ) _____ .

5. One's total surroundings are called one's ( ) _____ .

6. The atmosphere in the library is ( ) _____ to learning;

    it can help ( ) _____ learning because few aversive stimuli are present.

7. The ( ) _____ stimulus had the sound of buzzing
    bees.

8. He became ( ) _____ of the tension in the room.

9. A person in a severe psychotic state who is at times split from

    reality is called a ( ) _____ .

10. A person who has an extreme preoccupation with an idea and an

    intense concern with tidiness is called an ( ) _____ -

    ( ) _____ .

(1) auditory	(6) environment	(11) paranoid
(2) aversive	(7) extrovert	(12) psychotic
(3) compulsive	(8) introvert	(13) reinforce
(4) conducive	(9) neurotic	(14) schizophrenic
(5) conscious	(10) obsessive	

Master Quiz: Chapter 2

Circle *only* the prefix in each of the following words; then write the meanings of the prefix in the blank.

Example: (sub)terranean: <u>under</u> the earth (terra firma)

Word (circle prefix)	Meaning
1. exodus	to move _____ or away
2. premature	_____ maturity (or ahead of its time)
3. atheist	_____ from knowledge of God or gods
4. non-denominational	_____ having a denomination (or organized group, usually religious)
5. contemporary	_____ present time, now
6. reiterate	to state _____
7. biped	animal with _____ feet
8. monophonic	_____ sound or channel
9. autocratic	_____ -ruled; dictatorial
10. transcend	to go _____ or beyond

Master Quiz: Chapter 3

Fill in blanks with prefixes or roots you have studied. Meanings are given below the blanks.

1. If you make a _____acle of yourself, you will _____matically
    (to look)   (self)
 jeopardize any marriage proposals.

2. The _____ -Atlantic _____ ion personnel voiced indifference to the
    (across)   (send)

 proposed pro _____ile plans.
                (to throw)

3. His _____ ue could drive a person into _____ mission.
    (one) (study)   (under)

4. The _____ stetrician _____ ed a _____-habit forming pill.
    (against)   (before) (write)   (not)

5. The term "manic- _____ ive" labels a person whose moods can
                    (down) (push)
 swing from unrealistic, wild elation to black despair.

6. The word element **vert** meaning "to turn" is used in _____ vert,
                                                            (with)

 _____ vert, and _____vert.
 (away)   (back)

7. Any _____ active changes are not ap _____ able in this case.
    (back, again)   (to fold)

8. The easily trans _____ ed stereo com _____ ents sell better than
                    (to carry)   (to put)
 the big sets all in one case.

9. If you _____ stain from criticizing your _____ ponent, you
    (away, away from)   (against)

 will lose the election; think how politics are con _____ ed.
                                                    (to lead)

10. The _____stantial evidence in _____ ated that she had been cap-
     (around)   (to speak)
 tivated by his charisma (charm—pronounced: ca-**riz**-muh).

Master Quiz: Chapter 4

A. You know that the spelling of various prefixes change or adapt to the root that follows. Give the meanings of the following prefixes, and fill in the blanks with the adapted form. Note first example.

1. a. **in-** means <u>not</u>

   b. Many people in the world are illiterate or_____ moral.

2. a. **ad-** means _____

   b. I will _____cede to your proposals if you will grant me an _____ lotment.

3. a. **in-** means _____(as well as "not")

   b. Take me to your_____ lustrious leader, whose _____pressive behavior I have read about.

4. a. **con-** means _____

   b. We were _____ leagues at the time, serving with the _____ mand-er.

5. a. **ex-** means _____ (often written e-)

   b. The meaning of the ___lection's outcome___ludes me.

B. Fill in blanks below as specified.

6. Circle the *root* in the following words and write the meaning of the root in the blank following:

   retention (root meaning) _____

   cognition (root meaning) _____

7. Effective learning techniques should include finding out *at once* whether you are on the right track; this is called getting _____

   _____ .

8. One effective method for finding out whether you are right or not is to use D_____ R _____ C _____.

9. It is very helpful to consciously _____ what you are trying to learn to what you already know.

10. When you see new words, try breaking them into manageable parts, or syllables; often you can recognize _____ and _____ that you have studied.

Master Quiz: Chapter 5

Underline at least two word elements (prefixes or roots) in each sentence; write in the meaning of the underlined word element. The number in brackets indicates total points possible.

Example: A scholarly mind is an essential pre<u>re</u>quisite for a <u>theo</u>-<u>logian</u>. (4)

pre—before

re—back, again

theo—god

logian—study of

1, 2. A sociologist attributed the reduced venereal disease rate to widespread use of prophylactics. (7)

3, 4. Astrologists are interested in both homogeneous and heterogeneous groupings of people. (4)

5, 6. Interplanetary space study-teams include both United States astronauts and Russian cosmonauts. (3)

7, 8.   The dermatologist gave the following prognosis: her hypersensi-
tive skin condition will worsen if not treated. (5)

9, 10. Graphoanalysis can aid a patient in gaining introspection; bio-
feedback training can help him learn new patterns of behavior. (4)

Master Quiz: Chapter 6

A word or word element is in bold type in each of the following sentences. Fill in the blank with the meaning of that word or word element.

1. Thanos means "death"; **eu**thanasia refers to_____death or mercy-killing.

2. To inter**rog**ate someone means to _____ him questions.

3. The **obituary** column lists death notices; obituary means literally to fall, or go _____.

4. **Statutory** means legalized or declared by law or statute; statute comes from the root **sta** meaning _____ .

5. The terms "conservativism" and "liberalism" may not have exactly the same meaning to various people, but the "ism" means:

   conservativism: _____ in conservative ideas, actions

   liberalism: _____in liberal ideas, actions.

6. An **inference** is a conclusion or result suggested from available facts; to **infer** means literally to _____ .

7. A **mnemonic** device is a _____ trick.

8. An **applicant** is _____ ; a de**press**ant is something that _____.

9. If you go in**cogn**ito to the party, chances are you won't be _____ _____ .

10. If someone is **detained**, he is _____.

Master Quiz: Chapter 7

1. Fill in blanks with meanings from list on the left:

    homonym: _____ a similar meaning

    synonym: _____ the same sound

    antonym: _____ an opposite meaning

2. Which word means the same as **iso-**: separate_____ or equal _____?

3. The initials D.D.S. stands for the _____ of _____
    _____ degree.

4. An Ed.D. is a _____ of _____ .

5. If someone is corpulent, he has a fat _____ .

6. If you empathize with someone, you have feelings that are similar
    _____ or different _____?

7. An antipathy for something is a feeling_____ it.

8. Pathology is the study of_____ .

9. If you refuse to buy anything from a certain store because you
    disagree with that store's policies, you are _____ -
    ing it.

10. An antitrust suit is a legal action brought _____ a monopo-
    ly or business.

Master Quiz: Chapter 9

1. **Mis-** means "not"; it also means "one who hates." So a misanthropist is one who hates _____. A misogamist is one who hates

   _____ .

2. Indefatigable has what word elements in it?

   Prefixes: _____ Root: _____ Suffix: _____

3. Genocide means _____.

4. An archeologist studies man's _____.

5. A philanthropist is a _____ who shows it by giving away lots of money.

6. The gestation period is the period of _____.

7. A society ruled by women is called a _____.

8. RADAR is an _____ that stands for Radio Detecting and Ranging.

9. You can make it clear to others that A.D. stands for _____

   _____ .

10. What are the roots in the following terms and what does each root mean:

Term	Root	Meaning
Renaissance		
Medieval		

Progress Sheet

Chapter:	Completed Chapter	Completed Master Quiz	Score (10 maximum each chapter)
1. Learn how to learn			
2. Break learning elements into manageable parts			
3. Consciously link the unknown to the known			
4. Get immediate feedback			
5. Practice frequently			
6. Reward yourself			
7. Use the best tools available			
8. Study the things you are most interested in first		(no quiz)	
9. Experiment with words—enjoy learning			

Completion date: _____

Comments:

Answer Key: Master Quizzes

Chapter 1:

1. (8) introvert
   (7) extrovert
2. (11) paranoid
3. (9) neurotic
   (12) psychotic
4. (2) aversive
5. (6) environment

6. (4) conducive
   (13) reinforce
7. (1) auditory
8. (5) conscious
9. (14) schizophrenic
10. (10-3) obsessive-compulsive

Chapter 2:

1. ex-	out
2. pre-	before
3. a-	away
4. non-	not
5. con-	with

6. re-	again
7. bi-	two
8. mono-	one
9. auto-	self
10. trans-	across

Chapter 3:

1. spectacle, automatically
2. trans-Atlantic, mission projectile
3. monologue, submission
4. obstetrician, prescribed, non-habit
5. depressive

6. convert, divert, revert
7. retroactive, applicable
8. transported, components
9. abstain, opponent, conducted
10. circumstantial, indicated

Chapter 4:

1. a. not
   b. illiterate, immoral
2. a. to, toward
   b. accede, allotment
3. a. into
   b. illustrious, impressive
4. a. with
   b. colleagues, commander

5. a. out of, formerly
   b. election's, eludes
6. ten: to hold, cogn: to know
7. immediate feedback
8. Data Retention Cards
9. link, connect
10. prefixes and roots
    (or suffixes, affixes)

247

Chapter 5:

1, 2: **sociolog**ist: society, study of
       attributed: to, towards
       reduced: back, to lead
       disease: down, away
       prophylactics: thoroughly

3, 4: **astro**pologists: stars, study of
       homogeneous: same
       heterogeneous: different

5, 6: **inter**-planetary: between
       astronauts: star
       cosmonauts: universe

7, 8: **dermatolog**ist: skin, study of
       prognosis: thoroughly, to know
       hypersensitive: very

9, 10: **grapho**analysis: write
       introspection: within, to look
       biofeedback: life

Chapter 6:

1. **eu-**: good
2. **rog**: to ask
3. **ob-**: down, away
4. **sta**: to stand
5. **-ism**: belief
6. **in-**: into, **fer**: to carry

7. mnemonic: memory
8. applicant; one who applies
    depressant: pushes down
9. known (recognized)
10. held down or back

Chapter 7:

1. homonym: the same sound
    synonym: a similar meaning
    antonym: an opposite meaning
2. **iso-**: equal
3. D.D.S.: Doctor of Dental Surgery

4. Ed.D.: Doctor of Education

5. corpulent: body

6. empathize: similar

7. antipathy: feeling against

8. pathology: study of disease

9. boycotting

10. antitrust: against a monopoly

Chapter 9:

1. misanthropist: one who hates man
   misogamist: one who hates marriage

2. Prefixes: **in-, de-**
   root: **fatig**
   suffix: **-able**

3. genocide: murder of a race or ethnic group

4. archeologist: man's past, beginning

5. philanthropist: lover of man

6. gestation: pregnancy, carrying the young

7. matriarchy

8. acronym

9. *anno domini,* in the year of our Lord

10. Renaissance **naiss**   birth
    Medieval   **medie**   middle

Index